A Cestrian Song

Explorations Within the Extraordinary Hinterland of Cheshire History

Eli Lewis-Lycett

Cestrian (ses-tre-an) - relating, or belonging to, the county of Cheshire.

Contents

Visit thelocalmythstorian.com for more

Introduction

I don't know the exact metre used to denote the moment at which a person comes to be intrinsically connected to a place, but for me, there was a moment in the winter of 2022 that felt very much like such a thing. I had been living in Cheshire for fifteen years at that point, having grown up in neighbouring Staffordshire, and had long since come to hold a genuine love for the history of my adopted county.

That winter I had been lucky enough to become the resident folklore columnist for *Cheshire Life Magazine* and I was out walking the ancient trackways nestled in the countryside of Vale Royal (as I often do) considering some of the area's lesser-known folklore for forthcoming features. As I walked, I happened upon an alignment I had never noticed before, set between the trackway from the village of Moulton and the spire of the church in nearby Davenham. Something about it drew me in. The present-day church was completed in 1870, a relatively recent date as Cheshire village churches go, but I knew the site itself had been a centre of worship for the better part of a thousand years. I followed the track on, through the fields that ran alongside the bypass, and on into a walled passage that brought me directly to the lych-gate of St. Wilfrid's church.

Turning to look back along the track that had delivered me, it struck me how that very route must have been used similarly for hundreds of years by villagers. In times of celebration, in times of war, and in distant times when such journeys would have been accompanied by a host of now long-lost local folklore, that route would have been imperative to the connection of local communities. It was a simple observation, but in the cool white glare of the late afternoon sun, it was an observation that struck some kind of internal chord for me. In my own way, I felt connected to something far greater than a simple pathway through the fields. This no longer felt like my adopted county, rather It felt like the place I belonged.

I will not be alone in enjoying such moments, but it is these instances of quaint acknowledgment that help expand the vision of Cheshire's rich and famous history into other, unfurling corners of fascination. Of all the counties in the north of England, Cheshire is that which general history fans will likely know most about, its sentinels being as they are, so easily recognised throughout the wider region. Deva Victrix, the Roman settlement which had been founded in the first century, would develop across several hundred years and as a result, has left a vivid and tangible legacy, not just in the city of Chester itself but throughout the county as a whole. Later, the Vikings would visit the county and view of local history, be they lost castles or murderous rebellions. Others, where matters such as rustic prophecy and local folklore are centre stage, will straddle the borders between history and the supernatural. All are stories that I feel are genially unique in both generation and execution to the county of Cheshire, and great examples of the history we often miss when beset with the traditional carousel of Roman walls and eighteenth century industrialism that can so often dominate our local guidebooks and media.

History is for all of us, but our local history is perhaps where we find our most genuine sense of connection, tradition, and appreciation for the quirks and idiosyncrasies that ultimately make us who we are. It has been a pleasure to bring these stories together across the last year or so, and it remains an incredible privilege to be able to share them with curiously minded history lovers, whether local or further afield. I sincerely hope you enjoy this collection, and should it in any way inspire the exploration of your own myriad of local history, wherever you are, then it will have been worth it all the more.

Eli Lewis-Lycett
Cheshire,
2023.

Blood In the Barley

The Hidden Story of the Vale Royal Rebellion

The Vale Royal rebellion is a medieval tale of murder, manipulation and struggle set amidst one of the most turbulent periods in all of English history. Yet it is only when we bring the contributing political factors, key players and major events of the story together as one, that we can really appreciate just what a remarkable piece of Cheshire history the story truly is.

Storm Born

There are certain characters and places that become unavoidable when writing about Cheshire history in the medieval period. Ranulf de Blondville, 6th Earl of Chester is a fine example of this, so broad was his influence during the thirteenth century. Vale Royal Abbey, in its own way, shares that level of prominence too. Its history is intrinsically bound to wider political and military events of the age and a fully realised history of the abbey would likely run into the thousands of pages, its unique bouquet of characters and events weaving throughout the story relaid in much the same manner as do the holes of the golf course that is set in the abbey grounds today. Down each, we may find a tale that sends us back in time, but most remarkable among them is surely that of the rebellion that took place against its abbot and brethren during the 1330s.

It is a story that provides us with a genuine insight regarding life during a unique period in English history, a time when the concerns of both the peasantry and the gentry were briefly aligned, making them unlikely bedfellows, united in opposition to an increasingly ambitious system of ecclesiastical rule that was busying itself deconstructing the established socio-economic order of the rural world.

I have written previously about the latter half of the fourteenth century and the events surrounding Dieulacres Abbey across the border in Staffordshire which set the scene for the murder of John de Warton. That account, taken together with this, could be seen as localised bookends to what should be considered to be one of the most turbulent centuries in all of medieval England. It is a mark of the times that the Vale Royal rebels didn't just air their grievances in hope of resolution. They would band together and stride out across country, hunting down their quarry. In the fields of Cheshire, they would burn the harvest and butcher the livestock. They would, more than once, commit murder.

It is a story that, across the years, has given fans of deep local history plenty of cause to marvel, but it is one that has never been anything like fully understood. Whilst we might know what the rebels did, we haven't yet known *how* they managed to do it. Hopefully, we will enjoy the journey to that particular destination here together; a journey that begins in the heart of our county, and in the founding of a building that was built upon the personal, holy vow of a king.

There is a foundation myth connected to Vale Royal Abbey that has been doing the rounds for the better part of 700 years. It tells of how during a storm in the English

Channel, the future King Edward I became so concerned for his life that he knelt upon the deck and amidst the whipping winds of the fray, pleaded for the Virgin Mary to lift his ship up and on to safety. If she did this, as such was Edward's eye for a deal, he would build in her honour the greatest abbey in all of England. Vow made, in an instant, the winds receded and the skies cleared, the king and his party sailing back to England on a restful sea - only to see that once safely ashore, the storm again gathered strength, smashing the empty ship to pieces in the bay.

The provenance of this story, as you might expect, has been questioned aplenty, with many observers assuming Edward's channel crossing to have been made on return from crusade in the early 1270s. This is a difficult date, as it would place the storm as happening several years later than the first charter mentioning the abbey came into existence (in the year 1270). For me though, Edward had plenty of cause to travel across the channel during the preceding decade and so the story should not be so easily dismissed.

The English-held region of Gascony in modern-day France had been under threat of invasion from the Iberian Kingdom of Castile pretty much constantly throughout the period. It was a situation that had encouraged a match to be made by Edward's father, the ruling King Henry III, for his son with Eleanor, half-sister of the Castilian king,

Alfonso X. A key part of the deal was that Alfonso would stop toying with his idea of invading Gascony, which then subsequently became part of the young Edward's marriage bounty. As such, it is probable that the abbey's eventual founding, around 1270, was indeed a result of Edward effectively doubling down on an insurance policy before his leaving for crusade - not on his return; a reaffirming of his pledge to the Virgin Mary from that storm in the English Channel years before, in hope of good fortune on his travels to the East.

Why Cheshire was picked for Edward's statement piece is also directly tethered to events in his younger life. His marriage endowment of 1254 included land in Ireland and Wales, but chief among his English gift was the Earldom of Chester - from which he would use the title 'Lord of Chester' until his ascension to the throne in 1272. He was known to have been genuinely fond of the county, visiting on multiple occasions, and later, Edward's son - the future King Edward II - would himself go on to be granted the Earldom. Chester, and Cheshire as a whole, was a place held dear in Edward's heart. That his great church project should be set within it, an altogether natural choice.

His abbey would be first built at Darnhall, a tiny Cheshire village near Winsford today, and a place likely known to the young Edward due to its hunting lodge, long popular with the Earls of Chester. This initial endeavour however would be beset with problems from day one. The first monks arrived in 1274, but no sooner had they put on their robes that difficulties arose with their estate, courtesy of fierce local contention regarding their new forestry rights, which the locals had had long held in tenure for themselves.

Such privileges were key factors in the foundation of an abbey, timber being a serious business concern in the 1300s. Whilst it was far from unusual to have such issues early on in the life of an abbey, perhaps the distinctly partisan nature of the unrest this caused in Darnhall should have been taken as a warning of things to come. This, together with a more general lack of suitability at the initial site for future building, meant that a rapid change of direction was needed, and in 1276 the decision was made to move the abbey to a new site five miles north, on the edge of the Forest of Modrem, near the village of Over. Foundation stones were then laid by King Edward himself on 13th August 1277.

Stood in the summer sun, his family at his side, and at last having come good on his vow, Edward would have been a proud man knowing that the stage was finally set for the construction of what was to be the greatest Cistercian church in all of Europe. Plans were already being drawn up for Vale Royal to directly rival Westminster Abbey in scale. The world around him, however, would have very different, and very bloody, ideas to the contrary.

War in the West

In the years following the Norman invasion of England, and the eventual settling of the conflict, attention would naturally turn to the war-band kingdoms of Wales. Despite repeated military action, come the early thirteenth century, the Kingdom of Gwynedd, based in North Wales and Anglesey, had not only survived but had come to establish itself as a genuine concern to the Marcher Lordships - independently marshalled areas originally set up from Chester to Hereford as a buffer zone to England, where local nobility would rule in the king's name. With the emergence of Llywelyn ap Gruffudd as leader in 1256, the problem of Gwynedd had brought such concern to the English that an agreement was brokered at Montgomery in 1267 which saw Llywelyn formally recognised as Prince of Wales. This agreement, however, was purely between Gwynedd and the Crown. Further south along the border, Llywelyn was still very much at war with the Marcher Lords.

Many had come to blame the escalating situation in Wales on the lack of decisive action undertaken by his father, and so upon coming to the throne himself, Edward had vowed to handle things very differently. All he needed was an excuse to get the ball rolling, and following a snub at Chester in 1275, where Edward had invited Llywelyn to personally pay homage and reconfirm his allegiances, the new king finally had cause to act. In 1277, the very year of his visit to lay the foundations at Vale Royal, Edward declared war.

The conflict would rumble on one way or another until December 1282, when Llywelyn was killed at the Battle of Orewin Bridge before Edward led an army into the heartlands of Gwynedd resistance in Snowdonia to cement his victory completely. His success would usher in the great building period in North Wales, during which many of the castles and towns we know today first came into being. For the fledgling abbey back in Cheshire, the conflict and its aftermath could not have come at a worse time.

That Edward had likely intended Vale Royal to be his final resting place is of little doubt. At the outset, more than 90 masons were working on the project. Designed by the highly respected church architect Walter of Hereford, the building was originally set to be almost 400 feet in length, with a central tower, 13 radiating chapels, and a 140 feet cloister. During the first 4 years of construction alone, more than 35,000 cart-loads of stone were brought in from the quarry at nearby Eddisbury, and vast timber clearances ordered throughout the nearby forests. In 1283, Edward had even donated a piece of the 'True Cross' to the abbey; that supposedly being the actual wooden cross on which Christ was said to have been crucified. With the building project in Wales now firmly underway however, its borders barely a day's ride from Vale Royal, the enthusiasm and readiness to spend that had initially been fostered onto the abbey just couldn't last. Funds originally earmarked for Vale Royal had already been diverted into the war effort, and so too now would be the tradesmen themselves. Slowly but surely, the builders and stone masons vanished from their work in Cheshire.

Now living with far more pressing matters than the security of his pet project, by 1290, Edward's patronage of the abbey seems to have become utterly absent. When Walter of Hereford went to claim his wages for the forthcoming year of his contract, Edward made it clear that there would be no more forthcoming once that particular payment had been met, stating directly that he was 'no longer concerned by the works at Vale Royal.' Word spread fast and soon the few remaining masons and labourers still working on the site would leave too for fear of absent wages. From that point on, devoid of the pomp and ambition so prevalent just 16 years earlier, Vale Royal Abbey would be in a state of perpetual existential crisis, fighting for its very right to exist.

Words of Refusal

The difficulties that had faced the project during its earliest years in Darnhall were born from the dissatisfaction of the locals concerning the rights latterly granted to the abbey, carved out in their minds at least, from what they had long seen as a fair suite of their own. It was a problem that would repeat itself to an even greater degree with the new abbey at Over. Forestry rights were, for institutions such as that as Vale Royal, a much-needed route to ready cash in the church coffers. For those they were taken from in the process, it represented a multifaceted, almost incalculable loss.

The forests of medieval England were filled with the source material on which life depended. Timber was used not only in construction and for the maintenance of homes, but the woodlands provided warmth in winter too. In addition, the rights of free warren in the forest covered the game living within. Now, not only had the very substance of life been transferred from the local population to the abbey, but anyone wishing to use the forest for their basic nourishment would have to pay for the privilege too.

There were also broader local changes, many of which came with intrusive personal implications. For the marriage of a daughter, for example, a fee or 'leyrwithe' was payable by the father, should the families concerned inhabit abbey land. Rarely possible in terms of coin, this facet of the law often resulted in villagers having to pay via services rendered on the land of the institution, taking years to pay off. In another classic move of the era, the villagers of Over would also lose their right to hold a weekly market to the abbey in 1280. Again, this meant that anyone trying to make a living locally, to sell produce or ale, was subjected to fresh taxation.

Understandably, local populations were rarely pleased when such a church was invested so near to home, and almost from the year of its founding, the villagers of Over and Darnhall had demonstrated an acute ability to protest. With Edward so intimately connected to the situation at the time, this gave more options for recourse than would normally be expected. Complaining directly to the king in 1278, bringing with them their scythes as symbols of their working, independent status, Edward had dismissed the locals directly, commenting how 'as villeins you have come and as villeins you shall return'. With this language, calling the locals 'villeins', Edward was making a direct statement that as far as he was concerned, they were now little more than serfs; forever tied to the land and those who owned it.

For the better part of twenty years from these initial protests, there would periodically arise campaigns of complaint, reaching something of a juncture in the year

1307, when having finally presented their grievances to the Chief Justice of Chester, the court simply moved to re-affirm the rights of the abbey. It was a response that lit a spark. By this time, villagers from outlying communities were also feeling the turn of the abbey's screw, with the confiscation of the Middlewich salt pits now also falling into the gift of Vale Royal. The abbey's instinct for survival, constantly directed to success by its early stewards, had brought about a robust attitude to business dealings and a range of heavyweight legal techniques that would prove increasingly useful in the years to come.

Come 1320 Edward was dead and his son, King Edward II, was now on the throne. As famine threatened the county, Vale Royal, long since cut from its regal umbilical, found cause to embolden its attitudes even further. Local activism was beginning to turn violent, Richard of Evesham, 4th Abbot of Vale Royal, had been promoted from within and was well versed in the objections of the locals, with records of the time noting how he had once had his horse shot from under him with arrows whilst employed in the collection of tithes.

An interesting aside regarding Richard of Evesham is that he was famed during his tenure as being a kind of spiritual beacon for the ghosts of dead monks who may have died without confession, abbey records noting how their apparitions would appear before him in search of safe passage to heaven. The stated rationale for his horse being shot from under him, however, the collection of 'tithes', was an altogether more earthly matter.

Representing one-tenth of an amount of produce, this system of taxation had been in use since the classical period throughout Europe, and having been established in England by King Ethelwulf in 855, by the 1300s it had come to represent a genuinely poisonous issue for land owners and tenants alike. A central pillar of government at a local level, there are still a number of tithe barns (huge structures used for housing the tithe produce of a parish) located across Cheshire today. As a tenant, the collection of tithes was a visible reminder of who was in charge.

For the local gentry, to whom the tithe was previously owed, it was an intolerable affront to their long-held local status. In the issue of tithe collection by Vale Royal, local gentry and peasantry had found something like a common bond - a sense of things being a lot better under the old regime; after all, these were families that, for better or worse, had held the local community together for the better part of two hundred years. It was only a matter of time until such grievances galvanised into something like a rallying cry and come 1321, local hostility to the abbey was beginning to bubble over, when a servant of the abbot found himself at the cutting edge, quite literally, of local sentiment, Ormerod's *Cheshire History* noting that;

The hatred which had long been cherished against the abbey by its dependents now began to manifest itself in the most violent manner, as early as 1321, in which year it appears that the monks who ventured to pass their consecrated limits were pursued by the Winningtons, Leghtons and Bulkeleys, and only saved their lives by flight; and in the same year, it appears the Oldyntons murdered John Boddeworth, a monk of the abbey, and played football with his head.

John Boddeworth, or John of Budworth, was murdered by a group of local families who then apparently took to playing football with his severed head! This is a fascinating passage, which clearly references the risks that monks of Vale Royal could face when leaving the safety of the abbey boundaries.

Things sure were getting gruesome in the countryside around Vale Royal and come 1322, a new abbot would arrive to oversee the task of getting the whole thing under control - a man who would come to find himself cemented at the heart of the abbey's bloody fourteenth century history; Abbot Peter.

Five years into his tenure, in 1327, and far from impressed with the local situation, Abbot Peter would mount the most grievous legal action yet in an attempt to eradicate any notions the locals had of further rebellion. He drew up a legal document known as a 'custumal' specifically for the lands of Darnhall and Over. The aim was to definitively outline the respective positions of both sides in relation to the rights of Vale Royal once and for all. Its creation would simply serve to escalate the situation towards new troublesome heights, and in the process, lock in the major players of the piece.

As a first response, the people of Darnhall and Over seem to have partnered a genuine faith in the county justice system together with an organised, strategic resistance. They agreed, for example, that none would become involved in the grinding of flour at the abbey mill, rendering its operation stale. They would also, as they could best foresee, look at ways of renting out land away from the abbot under their own steam, casting flies into the ointment of any fresh economic plans he might have been working on. When Abbot Peter looked to punish them in return, they refused to acknowledge his authority to do so and demanded a trial by a jury made up of their neighbours and peers; something which would virtually guarantee their acquittal.

In 1336, the villagers combined again, this time to approach the Chester Justice with a claim that, due to an ancient Royal Charter which guaranteed their local rights and privileges, the abbey's actions over the preceding half century had all been in ill faith, if not outright illegal. Returning home after the hearing, their complaint refused again, they then instructed a delegation to meet directly with the king whilst he was travelling across the region.

Rounded up and imprisoned in Nottingham, the villagers were released when they somehow managed to pay a fine. And it is here our real questions start. You have to wonder just how were a group of locals from small, rural Cheshire communities managing to do all of this; mustering, travelling, and pursuing official routes of legal recourse? Not to mention having the financial clout to pay the fines that came their way in the process. It is inconceivable that the group would have had anything like the finances to pursue such campaigns alone, and even if they did, to have the influence and power to be taken seriously?

No, a common cause may have united them, but somewhere, someone of considerable means was deliberately directing events. Who this person was is a question we might better consider when we arrive at the most astonishing stage of the feud, and a series of events unrivalled in our local history for their sheer jaw-dropping audacity.

A Murderous Journey

From the custumal of 1327 and its resulting fallout, the feud between Vale Royal and the locals roared on unabated.

Petitions, refusals, assertions of rights, and attempts at retribution litter the record deep into the 1330s. This is an England fraught with fear of uprising, at continued war with Scotland, and about to embark on the conflict with France that would come to be known as the Hundred Years War. It is against this backdrop that the events of 1336 played out.

Abbot Peter had been in-situ for more than 15 years, and animosity on both sides was at an all-time high. It was at this point that further significant events took place that would ramp up the toxicity of the stand-off once more. In early 1336 the abbot had moved to deny the villagers of Over rights of burrage in the newly chartered local borough. Creation of burrage plots was the process of formally inclosing land around the villages, with this subdivision then in turn allowing new rights and workings to be extended upon it. It would seem the abbot had taken it upon himself to formally confiscate land that was still in dispute with the locals or, at the very least, deny them any ability to rent it out from the abbey directly.

Either way, it was a further slight to any lingering notions of power the locals may have still harboured. In large part, to rent a burrage, a tenant would need to be acknowledged as a 'freeman'; something that would be in direct opposition to the villein status deferred onto the locals and which the abbey constantly relied on when finding itself the subject of legal challenge; a process that Abbot Peter was more than comfortable in undertaking.

He was, by all accounts, a studious and meticulous man. Besides the issuing of the custumal, he is also believed to have been the guiding light behind the creation of the *Ledger Book of Vale Royal*, an internal chronicle from which so much history of the period has come to be drawn. Not only does the ledger chart a history of the abbey but contains within it a useful compendium of pleas, evidence, bulls, and grants charting the later medieval period at breadth. It is in the ledger that we find many of the recordings made regarding the actions of the villagers and, in turn, the abbey's response.

Whilst naturally vital to our understanding, we must remember that such works are duty-bound to contain a healthy degree of bias. It is the fact that the ledger is so comparatively open to read irrespective of this that makes it the gem it is.

June 1336 brought a fresh opportunity for Abbot Peter to deal a blow to his tormentors. Visiting King Edward III at his hunting lodge in King's Cliffe, Rutland, he appealed directly for assistance in his subjection of local disquiet back in Cheshire. As he left the meeting in the late evening, passing through the village of Exton with his groom, he would have been beginning his journey home no doubt hopeful of positive outcomes regarding the conversations that he had undertaken that day with the king. It would have been quite the shock then, when looking up in the fading light, he spotted on the road ahead the very band of locals he had been telling Edward about earlier that day.

More than one hundred miles from home, the gang had been lying in wait for him all day. Studying their faces at a distance, looking for signs as to their intentions, the abbot's gaze would have been drawn to the specific figure of a man he had come to know intimately across the timeline of his struggle, a landowner from Cheshire to which he had recently issued legal proceedings - William de Venables of Bradwall.

The Venables' were a proud Cheshire family. Beginning their line in England at the point of the Norman Conquest with Gilbert de Venables, they had been created Barons of Kinderton during the late eleventh century, as the Earl of Chester looked to start afresh following the destruction of the Harrying. William de Venables, now holding lands stemming from an inheritance he received during the 1280s, effectively a second stem of the Baronial family line, was a powerful and notable foe.

Before the abbot had time to comprehend what was unfolding before him, an arrow cut through the air and sunk into the chest of his groom, William Fynche. The rebels had done the unthinkable, and it seems de Venables himself was just as shocked as Abbot Peter at the sight, as upon seeing Fynche dying on the grass, he turned and fled in panic. The abbot, not one to shy away from a physical confrontation any more than he was a legal one, held his staff tightly and braced himself as the rebels rushed toward him. Just as he began to swing his staff in defence, the sound of hooves thundered up along the road behind him.

It was Walter le Walche (Walter the Welsh), cellarer of Vale Royal, who had been temporarily delayed with some other servants prior to the abbot's departure. Racing at full speed to the abbot's aid, the fiery monk charged into the rebel group, sword drawn, the ledger book recording how le Walche;

> *…charged in like a champion sent from God to protect his house and his father and felled those sacrilegious men to the earth, and left all those whom he found in that place half dead, according to the law of the Lord.*

In the chaos that followed, the rebels found themselves being chased down by the abbot's men; but all was not lost. Suddenly joined by a party of Rutland locals, they then turned back toward the abbot, overwhelming him and his party. The group then marched the abbot and his servants on to the nearby town of Stanford, in order to seek the council of the king themselves. Quite what they were expecting to happen once there is unclear, but next morning, the abbot and his men were duly released, whilst those that had brought them to heel were in-turn placed in chains.

In the immediate aftermath, supporting detail appears to have been given to the king concerning the entrenched, mitigating factors of the feud, as incredibly, the rebels were soon released themselves, together with an order for Abbot Peter to return to them any goods he had taken from them in the run-up to the skirmish. The incident raises again some serious questions as to the method of the organisation behind the rebel group. To have been able to track the abbot across country, substantial assistance and provision would have been required. One hundred miles is at least a four-day trip by horse. That's four days of food and water for a group of six men and their horses.

Furthermore, they will have needed to be guided, literally, to know precisely where the abbot would be on the night of the attack. The sudden arrival of locals to help their plight would too suggest a strong local connection somewhere in the background.

The naming of de Venables might help us in our pursuit of understanding, the ledger book sharing two key accounts concerning the de Venables family from the time of the fight at Exton. First is a direct reference to the killing of the abbot's groom and of how de Venables fled the scene, where we are told that William;

...took to flight and did not dare to stay his foot till he came to parts of Cheshire, and he abandoned those he brought with him, and never looked behind him.

Combined with the following recording of legal action concerning the de Venables family in an evidence entry of 1337, we can start to get a real feeling for the situation at hand;

Be it remembered that in the year of our Lord 1337, in the vill of Merton, this agreement was made between the abbot and convent of Vale Royal on the one part and Thomas de Venables, son of William de Venables, on the other part, in the presence of Monsieur Hugh de Venables, Sir John de Arderne and Sir Periz de Thornton and others. Whereas the said Thomas challenged and claimed for himself and Aleyne, his wife, inheritance belonging to the land which he held in the lordship of Budworthe, next the pool of Darnhale in consequence of the overflow of the water on his land aforesaid, a fishery which he has used for a long while by force and arms, contrary to peace. And it was thereupon agreed between the parties that the abbot should take an oath with five of his counsel that he had done no wrong to the said Thomas, but had used his right in the manor of Darnhale, belonging to his church of Vale Royal, as the king had given

*to him and his predecessors, abbots of that place, at the first
foundation of their abbey. And after this the said Thomas
offered to the abbot £20 for his amends. And likewise, the
said Thomas de Venables solemnly took his oath that never,
with nets or in any other way, would he fish in the abbot's pool
of Darnhale, however much the water might overflow, and
would do no other harm to the abbot or his people, either
himself or through his people. And whereas the said Thomas
had wounded John de Eynesham, monk of Vale Royal, and
had taken from him and from his servants bows, arrows,
swords and other things contrary to right, he pledged him
100s for his amends, and would give him a suitable bow
with the arrows belonging, or a sole sparrow-hawk. And also
the said Thomas pledged half a mark to John Hele, whom he
had beaten against the peace…and the knights above named,
that is to say, Monsieur Hugh, Sir John and Sir Periz, who
came with the said Thomas de Venables, undertook that the
said Thomas should keep these covenants in all things, and if
not then the said lords will utterly cease to maintain the said
Thomas, and will maintain the said abbot against him.*

This action 'being remembered' in 1337 would suggest
this came to pass after the events in Rutland took place. In
it, we learn of how (spoiler warning) yet another dispute
between long-held rights, in this case, the fishing rights of
Darnhall, were being contested between a local man -

Thomas de Venables, son of the William mentioned in our Rutland attack - and the abbey.

Petty? Maybe, but let us look at the severity of the address granted; a fine issued against de Venables and oaths taken by witnesses confirming that they would side with Abbot Peter in future disputes over the issue. We also learn that Thomas de Venables had apparently wounded another servant from the abbey and stolen his weapons, and had also beaten a man called John Hele. Taken together, this information places the de Venables family squarely at the heart of the local rebellion. The son, an infamous local figure for the abbey's ongoing concern, and the father personally present at the killing of the abbot's groom in Rutland.

By 1337 then, we have a picture fast coming into focus of how long, tired and bitter feuds between the local gentry and the abbey have turned into open violence, with the de Venables family of Bradwall at centre stage. William de Venables appears to have been the man that had mustered locals to journey across the breadth of England to attack the abbot on his return from Kings Cliffe in 1336, and now a year later, an agreement is being made before the local justice regarding the fining of his son Thomas, who by all accounts seems quite the handful himself. Likely, the wording of the action against Thomas would have been intended to mark an end to the disagreements, but as we will see, the campaign against Abbot Peter was far from over.

In the same year, we see just how broad a distance the abbot's trials had taken him when a situation arose between a Sir William de Clifton, connected to Kirkham in North Yorkshire, and the priory of the same name, which had been brought into Vale Royal's concern toward the end of the previous century. A dispute had broken out regarding Abbot Peter's refusal to sell the rights of tithe collection to de Clifton in respect of the village of Wetsby; a hotly contested corner of the priory's Yorkshire estate. To spite the priory, and therefore Vale Royal, de Clifton had deliberately let the produce stored in the Wetsby tithe barn waste away and rot, setting out the priory's share in a local rectors cart, where it sat in the middle of a field for a month as his tenants chased off anyone who attempted to collect it. Furthermore, he vigorously contested any attempts by the abbey to punish any tenants that had carried out actions on his orders, personally beating a servant of the priory before a crowd at Preston and being excommunicated as a result.

The depth of the abbot's notoriety in Cheshire was not, it seems, without its refractions in both Lancashire and Yorkshire too, such was the realm of the abbey's estates. The cauldron of vitriol that was boiling away concerning the abbot and his mission was reaching its climax, and in the last year of the decade, it would finally explode.

The Year of Burning

 Far from a group of local peasants rebelling against the will of an oppressive abbey, we have come to learn that the relentless air of insurrection, so long encapsulating the story of Vale Royal in the 1300s, was most likely born from the reactions and manipulations of the local gentry. Keen to protect their interests, reeling against the gifts bestowed upon the abbey in its early years, they were, and perhaps justifiably so in the context of the age, enraged by the changing world around them.

   In an England full of conflict and political flux, only recently rebuilding from the somewhat disastrous reign of King Edward II - who had fallen from power amidst tension with his wife Isabella and her lover, Roger Mortimer - the concerns of local land disputes were often deemed to be matters that began and ended with the word of local county justice. Influence upon the purveyors of that justice, therefore, was exerted and expected in equal measure. The king, now hard at work seeking to reassert control over the regions his father had so neglected, was as keen as any to let such matters simply resolve themselves, and at Vale Royal, things were about to do just that.

Throughout 1339, raids on the fields and barns of the abbey had increased, with crops burned, livestock killed and several abbey buildings destroyed. There was a real drive now, delivered by the locals, powered by the de Venables family, to force an untenable situation upon Abbot Peter and his brethren. Between the smouldering fields and the ox blood running in the streams, and given the violence and malefactions that awaited the abbey's servants on the roads, there must have been an assumption that surely, amongst the destruction, Abbot Peter would be finally forced to relent in his quest for the abbey's continual advancement. That he would, at last, get the message. He did not and so, the final act of his story was written.

Sometime after August 1339 (the date of his last entry in the ledger) we know that both Abbot Peter and his champion protector, the sword-wielding Walter le Walche, were murdered on abbey land somewhere near modern-day Davenham. Being logical, that they were caught up in a raid on the abbey just before harvest time, at the end of September, is a fine fit for the timeline. This event, the coup de grace of our piece, is recalled in the ledger book during February 1344; the perpetrators of the day having finally been called to account.

It reads;

Be it remembered that on the Ides of February (13th)

1344, in the monastery of Vale Royal, Thomas de Venables, Alan son of Alan le Noreys, William son of Ralph de Bostok, Robert son of Thomas de Acton and Roger de Hulgreue, present in person, satisfied the abbot and convent of the said monastery for the death of Lord Peter, the late abbot, and Brother Walter le Walche, a monk of the said monastery, and for other trespasses and injuries inflicted upon the said abbot and convent and their monastery, in this manner: to wit, that the aforesaid Thomas, Alan, William, Robert and Roger, will do and procure to and for the said abbot and convent in being, and for the time to come, and their monastery, all the good which they can do and procure, as well in the persons of themselves and their tenants, as in all their goods and chattels whatsoever, so long as they shall live. Each of them, moreover, will give so long as they shall live, every year on the day of the death of the aforesaid Lord Abbot Peter, less they be lawfully prevented (and, if so prevented, then on another day in the same year), two pounds of wax to the light of Blessed Mary of the monastery aforesaid. And to do the same faithfully and observe them firmly, the aforesaid Thomas, Alan, William, Robert, and Roger, having touched the holy gospels, took their corporal oath in the presence of the venerable father Roger, Lord Bishop of Coventry and Lichfield, the abbot and convent of the said monastery, and other trustworthy witnesses.

Rather than a direct blood punishment, this entry records a particularly curious agreement between the parties involved. Along with Thomas de Venables, the group called to the abbey to account for the deaths of Abbot Peter and Walter le Walche are all members of the local gentry. Alan le Noreys is noted in records of the period as a 'lord of Speke' whilst William de Bostok held smallholdings in the local area, and we should assume the same too of de Acton and Roger de Hulgreue. Together with a general agreement that all would now do their best by the abbey, there is a mandate that all should, on the anniversary of Abbot Peter's death 'give two pounds of wax to the light of Blessed Mary of the monastery'.

At first, from my research, I had thought this is a form of penance, the group needing to observe and prey for Abbot Peter for the duration of the candle's burning. This would likely take more than two hundred hours to complete, however, and so unlikely to be the true meaning of the agreement. Rather, I find it probably a literal request for two pounds of wax to be contributed to the lighting of a candle in the abbey itself. Beeswax was the preferred light fuel of choice during the fourteenth century due to its clean, sweet smell and was incredibly expensive, perhaps making it a relatively fitting fine, especially when expected every year, for life.

That the culprits associated with Abbot Peter's death did

not come together at the abbey until early 1344, more than four years after the likely date of the murder, is probably a function of external pressures finally coming to bear on their reputations and families. That is to say, such were the difficulties and confusions surrounding the situation in late 1339 that it may well have taken several years for threats and litigation to bind themselves together in such a manner as to make the hearing unescapable.

That no one was then imprisoned, let alone executed for the murder, could actually be one of our most telling insights regarding the feud. To me, it denotes an absence of sympathy toward the abbey from Crown and local justice alike. That there might have been a collective sigh of relief by all involved that Abbot Peter, with his relentless force of will and fiercely stubborn thinking, had finally, if bloodily, been removed from the equation, is not an unreasonable thought at all. Unwilling to play politics with any constructive consideration, such an end had perhaps even become considered inevitable.

As we have seen throughout the lifetime of the feud, particularly with the murder of William Fynche at Exton back in 1336, this is not an age of rock-solid legal recoil for the local gentry and nobility. That the villagers of Over and Darnhall, however so guided, were prepared to resort to violence in an attempt to settle their disputes with Abbot Peter should be held against the perspective reality of the situation. Before the events at Exton had sparked the fire that would untimely lead to the abbot's murder, those villagers had, through avenues of both county justice and the Royal court, attempted more than a dozen times to get suitable assistance from the authorities of the land. These attempts had been shaped, funded, and encouraged by those members of the local Cheshire gentry that also had their own private issues with the way the abbey was enforcing its newly granted rights and privileges.

Without the gentry being so motivated, it is unlikely that we would know anything about these events today. Our story would simply have never come to pass. It is far from an unrealistic view that figures of the local gentry like de Venables had struck a deal with the muscle of their local communities in return for funding and legal advice in their own endeavours. Regarding Abbot Peter, for all the temptation that may be offered enticing us to view him as something of an ecclesiastical tyrant, he was in all probability simply acting in a way that he saw to be his duty, seeking to secure the future of his community and house.

Undoubtedly both he and de Venables were formidable men of their times, and if their actions may look primarily self-serving to us today, neither should be seen as wholly good or bad. In many ways, they were both victims of circumstance, each vying for the right to influence the world around them in an attempt to better ends; the expectations of their followers, friends, and family, would have been no less burdensome for either. Vale Royal's immediate future would see it navigate the Black Death of the late 1340s and on toward an England in which, courtesy of the damage done by the plague, those villagers, tenants, and workers that had proven to be thorns in the side of its ambitions thus far, would briefly come to hold unprecedented powers. The labour required for institutions such as Vale Royal to thrive had always been a question of community cooperation on one level or another.

Working the fields, the forests and the farms was a manual, backbreaking role, without which, any notion of wealth and influence for those running the land could be cast into the dirt. With such drastically reduced numbers available for work post-pandemic, local labour prices would sore to the point that the abbey's very survival was wholly dependent on the investment of local workers. As a result, although it may have changed shape and colour in the process, the embittered relationship between Vale Royal and its surrounding communities would continue long into the second half of the fourteenth century.

Vale Royal Abbey was founded ready-forged with the greatest of ambitions courtesy of its direct Royal patronage. It is hard to believe now as we look back that this fusion was ever going to lead to anything other than the most troubled of journeys. Events of the late thirteenth century conspired to mean that its initially declared destiny, as the greatest abbey in England, would never come to realisation. Yet that sense of what could still be, of what was *supposed* to be, would drive the abbey along a unique path and one - that for those connected to it - could just as easily lead to destruction as it could prosperity.

The tale of our local rebellion is filled with the fires, murders, and riotous indignation that would come to typify much of the period when it came to the conflict between the Church and the gentry. It is one of the most remarkable Cheshire histories and one that prompts deeper questions too. Be it Abbot Peter, Thomas de Venables, Vale Royal itself, or even those members of the forgotten cast acting as ghosts in the shadows of the feud, both blame and praise prove harsh mistresses to all when it comes to the conflicting motivations jostling at the heart of the tale.

All are characters that we have remembered only due to the parts they played in a story when, briefly, they found themselves standing in opposing positions on the central, brutal stage of the most turbulent period of later medieval England. There is surely potential to find a little of both Abbot Peter and de Venables in all of us, and I wonder which side we would have found ourselves on, quite involuntarily, had we been residents of Cheshire all those years ago.

Beneath the brutality and frustration, this is a story that

may also offer us the chance to spot the morphic echo that would go on to form a buttress to the arc of Cheshire's greater history across the following 400 years; the fighting truth of Cheshire's independent spirit. Recast in the colours of armed rebellion, continental and civil war alike, it is this facet of the Cestrian nature that would inform the key equations of England's most powerful families for long years beyond the blood of Abbot Peter spilling out across the harvest fields of Vale Royal.

There are other uprisings of course, other bitter feuds, and plenty of hated abbots peppering the ledgers, chronicles, and ballads of medieval England, but in any other county, we could not have had the particular blend of circumstances needed to create such a tale as ours. We could not have the king and his grand abbey project, nor the wars hovering on the border that ruined its ambitions, but perhaps most crucially of all, given the royal patronage of the county at large that had so emboldened the local gentry across the preceding centuries, only in Cheshire could we find such a fierce sense of independence coupled with the requisite gumption to ensure the historical powder-keg on hand would so vividly ignite.

Perhaps more than any other, the Vale Royal rebellion truly is a tale all of our own, it being without a genuine comparable elsewhere in the history of England; in the purest of senses, it is a true Cestrian song.

Invisible Fortress

The Vanishing of Shipbrook Castle

The castle at Shipbrook near Davenham is long lost to us today, its last traces being cleared from the land in the 1790s. However, in balancing the brutal events of early Norman England together with the history of a key local family, not only can we better appreciate this often overlooked corner of medieval Cheshire, but perhaps for the first time, look to understand the story of Shipbrook Castle and its ties to a bloody revolt against King Henry IV.

A New Technology

What do you think of when images of historical England are brought to mind? For many of us, few things better represent the distinct charm and lure of English history than the image of the castle. Imposing in construction and romantic in ruin, the castle offers a tangible connection to both the history and accompanying fantasy of the medieval world. The gatehouse, the keep, the moat, and the towers; all are easy images to drum up. These great fortresses have played host to kings, queens, rebellion, and battle, if more recently primarily finding their audiences in those visitors enjoying a historical day out.

The castle is the one historical structure that everybody you know will recognise, irrespective of their interest, or lack therefore, in history as a whole. This is true in most part for the wider world as well. It is the castles that draw the more inquisitive visitors from the US, Japan, and Australia, whereas our great palaces tend to cater for those with a majority interest in British history that lies in the more personal trials and tribulations of the Royal Family. Nothing wrong with that of course, but I can't imagine they'll come across too many oubliettes.

In reality though, our castles are far more than mere

agents of the period in which they were built, which in itself is a complex issue. Castles are often built on sites with a defensive legacy stretching back into the time of the Anglo-Saxons; a time that is as distant to those who laid their foundations as they are to those who bore witness to the events that would ultimately place them in ruin.

Those with an interest in such topics as that of the castle will appreciate that the grand structures of Warwick and Windsor are rarified examples. Most are tumbling, blow-hole-laden vestiges of all we imprint onto them in our minds. For the most part, a visit to an English castle, or a Welsh one for that matter, will bring far more by way of knee-high ruined walls, floor plan information boards, and cannon-blasted crumbled towers than it will anything classically grandiose. And that of course, is the biggest part of their charm. If walls could talk, our decaying, elemental castles would shout across the fields of events we can barely conceive.

Throughout Cheshire, we are blessed with a startling array of castles to visit and study, primarily due to the county being one of the original administrative centres of England established by the Norman regime following their victory at Hastings in 1066. Before the Norman conquest, when William, Duke of Normandy landed at Hastings in order to claim the throne of England, the Anglo-Saxons had their strongholds, but they weren't like our traditional castles in their aesthetics. These were much broader defensive structures, built around communities as a whole, sometimes along the lines of earlier Roman fortifications. Founded primarily under the rule of Alfred the Great, these *burhs* have survived in administrative terms to give us many of our 'borough' borders today.

Castles, as we have come to know them, find their origins in Europe during the tenth century, and it was this new style of fortification, employed to establish control of an area both militarily and economically at speed, that would provide William of Normandy, latterly William the Conquerer, with the key tool for the cementation of his rule in England. Built in large numbers across the Saxon landscape to provide immediate protection from, or perhaps more importantly, to promote the subjugation *of*, rebellious local populations, the castle was crucial to the success of the new Norman regime.

Far from the classic image we have today, these early constructions were primarily formed of an earthen mound (motte) and protected courtyard (bailey), all of which would then be surrounded by a further protective ditch and palisade wall. They were cheap to construct and quick to build. The perfect 'pop-up' defensive site. Around a thousand were built in the aftermath of the invasion and for the existing population in the settlements around them, they constituted a new and frightening concept; especially when reinforced with a stone keep atop their central mound. From their beginnings in earth and timber, some would go on to find themselves decommissioned whilst others would grow into stunning examples of stone-built engineering. Later, as their benefits became increasingly evident, more and more castles were built in stone from the off; which together with their earlier Norman counterparts give rise to the suite of fortifications that we now have available throughout the country as a whole.

Stronghold Cheshire

In the years following the conquest, Cheshire would be cast as a frontier region, a swell of land keeping Norman England from the warring, neighbouring kingdoms of Wales. It is no fluke that of the twenty castle sites located in the county, nine are found within just a few miles of the Welsh border.

Our earliest strongholds are found at Chester, Frodsham, and Halton. All were originally constructed shortly after the Norman conquest circa 1070, their differing fortunes across the years illustrating well the diverse manner of destiny for the castle at large. Chester is still very much a feature of the city centre today thanks to its conversion to stone during the twelfth century and the fact that it came to play a prominent part in our national history during the years that followed. The list of prominent prisoners held at Chester throughout its time reads like a roll call of England's later medieval history; King Richard II, Andrew de Moray, and John Neville plus many more spent significant time within the crypt of the Agricola Tower.

Frodsham was never converted to stone, and had fallen into disrepair come the 1300s, with modern interpretations of the castle coming from the fortified manor house that replaced it. Halton sits somewhere between the two. With roots as a pre-historic defensive site, it enjoyed a busy history from its inception right up to the Civil War period, and although now ruinous, its refurbishment in sandstone during the thirteenth century means that a good portion of physical evidence remains on site today; a later courthouse built in the 1700s surviving completely intact and now serving as the Castle Hotel.

I share these examples to show how no matter the strength of the classic image, that popular, a-typical, vision with its great walls and stone towers is in fact, for the most part, a historical trick-of-the-light. It is a snapshot, frozen in time, surviving into the modern age by way of private conservation and national schedule, representing an ideal of time and place. As such, they are vital bastions of legacy, providing a clear and defined portal through which we can view the past, but we should always try to remember that no matter how awe-inspiring these stone castles may be, they serve to show only one part of a far greater tale. For every great castle still with us today, there are a dozen that have long since vanished. Some by way of war, but just as many, by fluke of economics and simple ill-fashion.

I've personally lost count of the number of times I've seen a Castle Street, Castle Hill, or Castle View with no sight of such a structure for miles around. Yet in most instances, on looking a little closer, such places tend to have certain details in common. They may be found on a modern street that follows the line of a Roman road or they may present to the world as a children's play area perched atop a conspicuous-looking hill. More elusive still, they may consist now of little more than a bumpy quarter of earth in an overgrown woodland, which only after careful study will reveal a commanding view of the land around it. It is one such place that we will explore in this piece, and one with a history so rich it should perhaps be considered as much a part of this county's heritage as any of its far more famous counterparts; the lost castle of Shipbrook.

From the nature of its purpose to its precise location, the history of Shipbrook Castle is shrouded in mystery. A significant part of this confusion is centred on an often-quoted academic view that, as with many castles built in Cheshire, Shipbrook was first constructed in response to the Norman-Welsh wars of the late eleventh and early twelfth centuries. This has held firm for the better part of seventy years, even though Shipbrook lies more than twenty miles away from the Welsh border and too far behind the Norman defensive network along the Dee to denote itself of practical use. My research into the castle will suggest something very different - and something much more personal to its founder.

There are significant clues as to the original purpose of the castle when we consider its location, which I will share now before further exploration of its history and custodians. Leaving the village of Davenham along Church Street, within a mile we reach Shipbrook Bridge, an ancient crossing over the River Dane, where today the river is in fast flow. As the land then rises gently beyond the bridge towards Shipbrook Hill Farm - once known in the local record as Castle Hill - there are clear markings on the land escapement as it arrives at the setting of the farm. These earthworks suggest a deliberately landscaped approach from the river. Visiting in person, the view from the farm too, back across the river towards the village of Davenham is completely befitting the strategic positioning that one would expect to find at such a site.

Corroboration of these observations comes from George Ormerod's immense 1882 work *The History of the County Palatine and City of Chester*, who states the last remains of the castle as having been cleared around 1790 to make way for the farm, which itself contains antiquated sandstone in its construction, suggesting a repurposing of masonry a-typical of sites which vanished throughout the period. This is important, as the fact that there was masonry present confirms that the castle was affluent enough to have been rebuilt in stone during its early history.

The key question of that history is why, when comparatively speaking the surrounding Cheshire landscape was chock-full of sites with clear and obvious military functionality, was a castle at Shipbrook needed at all? What was it like? And what of its stewards? I promise, far from the less noteworthy ends met by some, the vanishing of Shipbrook is a remarkable and bloody tale - and it begins with the brutal events that took place across the county during the winter of 1069.

The Harrying

Twenty years after the Norman conquest of 1066, King William required some financial understanding. To properly assess the wealth of his new kingdom, to tax it, he commissioned a great survey, sending riders out to every corner of England to collect information on everything from livestock and plough-hands to bridges and slaves; the results of which were bound together for eternity in that now world-famous tome, *Domesday Book*.

Although the hamlet of Shipbrook is today considered to be a part of Davenham, at the time of the great survey it was valued independently and was found to be worth double the income of its neighbour with an 'annual value to the lord' of 10 shillings. The settlement consisted of 2 villagers, 2 slaves, and 2 plough teams. At this point, in 1086, the manor of Shipbrook was in the possession of Richard de Vernon, who had been awarded a suite of lands at the expense of the local Saxon Lord Osmer following the division of holdings across Cheshire that took place in the wake of the conquest.

What is most telling from the entry relating to Shipbrook, and key to Richard de Vernon's founding of the castle, is spotting just how much Shipbrook's annual revenue had sunk during the twenty years since the Norman takeover, its previous annual value being placed at the quite considerable figure of 1 pound; double what it was worth in 1086. It is a similar story in Davenham too, with an annual value that almost halved during the same period, and indeed so is the case with the nearby manor of Leftwich. All are signs of the dreadful situation that had arisen in the north of England across the period.

By the winter of 1069, more than three-quarters of the population of northern England had either been killed or exiled during a campaign of brutal savagery waged by the new king in what has become known to history as the Harrying of the North. Virtually all settlements across what we now think of as Cheshire, Derbyshire, and Staffordshire, had been desolated during the campaign as William looked to rid his kingdom of the rebellious northern populations that were proving so troublesome to the completion of his plans.

The rebellion had started in Northumbria, partly as a reaction to the way Norman rule had affected its people during William's absence in 1067. His return home to France had seemingly taken any notion of concern for the population of England with it, and those that had been charged with ruling while he was away had taken up the dark arts of raping and pillaging with a terrible gusto. As the rebellion gathered pace through 1068 it morphed into a full-on counterclaim to the throne, rallying behind Edgar Ætheling, the last heir of the deposed House of Wessex, and a figure to whom the conquered people of England felt they could turn in a bid to restore the normalities of life lost since the conquest.

This wasn't an altogether spurious ambition. At the start of William's consideration of the campaign he had sent a force of 900 Norman soldiers into the town of Durham in order to secure the peace. Just two made it out alive. Come 1069, the future of England was seriously in the balance as rebellions began to surface across the Midlands too. William needed to act.

Entering the fray directly, he took to crushing revolts across the country in a game of bloody whack-a-mole that was threatening his grip on the crown; something exacerbated further still when, that autumn, the King of Denmark landed in support of the northern uprising. William raced to York to meet the Danish force and in time-honoured tradition, when it came to appealing to those known as 'Danes', paid them gold and silver to return home. Once they left, he vowed to hunt down the indigenous leaders of their would-be northern alliance. The problem was though, try as he might, he simply could not find them.

The rebel's success had largely been found in their ability to operate a gorilla war, attacking quickly, and retreating into the countryside. Frustrated and tired by their elusive nature, William decided he would lay waste to the North in totality, removing any ability the rebels had to feed themselves let alone rally further banner-men. Settlements, livestock, crops, absolutely everything would burn, and nothing was off limits for the perversions of the soldiers carrying out his orders. It was, some modern observers have suggested, an English genocide. Just how savage this campaign was is illustrated well in the writings of those who documented early Norman rule, as whilst naturally biased and supportive of the new regime, even they found themselves unable to hide their true feelings regarding the levels of barbarity that had been poured onto the people of the land. Writing fifty years after the event, the Anglo-Norman chronicler Orderic Vitalis stated how;

> *The king stopped at nothing to hunt his enemies. He cut down many people and destroyed homes and land. Nowhere else had he shown such cruelty. This made a real change. To his shame, William made no effort to control his fury, punishing the innocent with the guilty. He ordered that crops and herds, tools, and food be burned to ashes. More than 100,000 people perished from starvation. I have often praised William but I can say nothing good about this brutal slaughter. God will punish him.*

Following the campaign, and particularly due to the scorched earth tactics employed during it, the value of land in northern England had been flawed. There was little fertile land left to cultivate crops, few animals left to care for, and a huge reduction in the number of people who were fit and able enough to conduct a labouring life. In the aftermath, Hugh d'Avranches, Earl of Chester and William's main man in the county, was charged with bringing about economic recovery in his local region.

The first step in achieving this would be the creation of

new Baronial titles, granted to those figures that d'Avranches could trust to manage their estates sympathetically to the cause. Richard de Vernon, a veteran of Hastings, was one of the men in line for such a title, and Shipbrook provided part of his administrative responsibilities in Cheshire alongside lands in Bostock, Crewe, Davenham, and Leftwich.

In such a ravaged world, practical value had temporarily shifted from the immediately obvious to the more strategic. It is in light of this, that from all the lands at his disposal, Richard de Vernon chose Shipbrook as his new Baronial seat. The position of the settlement, overlooking a crossing on the River Dane, would have made Shipbrook his most valuable asset. Control of such a river crossing meant control of trade. As such, a fortification at Shipbrook would have been necessary almost immediately.

History Makers

From their base at Shipbrook, the Vernon family would begin a regional dynasty that would see their name etched into the history of both Cheshire and Derbyshire to such an extent that any visit we make today to a local historical site, country house, cathedral, or even large parish church, is more often than not accompanied by the Vernon coat of arms being proudly displayed somewhere in the vicinity.

The family's roots may have been back in the Eure region of Normandy, but their Cheshire holdings had given them such a foothold in the new kingdom that they would help shape the fortunes of not just the county, but of wider English history across the centuries to come.

Richard de Vernon would go on to marry Adzelia, daughter of William Peverel (reputedly an illegitimate son of William the Conqueror himself) and would then become an advisor to William's son, King Henry I, during the difficult early years of his reign. So close did Richard become to the new king that he was often the sole signatory to Henry's charters and decrees. As a result, come his death in 1107, Richard had expanded his personal empire significantly, acquiring lands as far away as Devon, Hampshire, and on the Isle of Wight. Shipbrook meanwhile, had become an established economic centre.

Over the following three hundred years, the castle would continue to prosper as the Vernon's influence grew throughout England as a whole, and it is likely that it is during this period, probably around the Welsh Wars in the 1280s, that Shipbrook was formally transformed into a stone fortress. As with many such families of the period, great power was often a source of political conflict and the fortunes of castles such as Shipbrook were only ever one twist of fate away from sudden decline. Throughout the thirteenth and fourteenth centuries, England was an incredibly turbulent place. The twelfth century civil war known today as The Anarchy - when the succession of the throne of Henry I was contested between his daughter, Empress Matilda, and his nephew, Stephen of Blois - saw conflict between various English barons and war leaders as the ruling classes of the nation picked their favoured side.

It is a conflict in which Hugh de Vernon, 3rd Baron of Shipbrook (1113-1165) would no doubt have had a role to play. The fourteenth century too, with the Black Death and the decimation it brought to the population of Europe, is likely to have killed around half of Cheshire's population, and the laws passed in its wake, designed to maximise economic governance, would have been a serious contention for people such as those living at Shipbrook Castle. But it would the fifteenth century, and its period of unprecedented Royal turmoil, that the defining moment for Shipbrook would arrive, with the first trials of that infamous conflict between the houses of York and Lancaster that would come to be known as the Wars of the Roses.

The Hotspur Revolt

The Percys were a powerful family from Northumberland and their lands formed an integral part of England's border defence against the Scots. They had long been staunch supporters of Henry IV and had played a vital role in the war with Richard II that had resulted in Henry taking the throne in 1399. The rewards for such support, as you might imagine, had proved considerable. Star of the family, Sir Harry 'Hotspur' Percy (so named for his speed in battle) had duly received numerous gifts and titles, not least amongst them the offices of High Sheriff of Flintshire and Justice of Cheshire. His ageing father, the Earl of Northumberland, may still have been head of the family, but there was no doubt as to Hotspur's new-found station amongst the elite. A personal favourite of the new king, for Hotspur, the future was bright. His new role in Flintshire was a timely appointment, North Wales now finding itself a hotbed of warring activity courtesy of the new rebel leader Owain Glyndŵr.

Glyndŵr represented a serious threat to the fledgling rule of Henry, and so it is a sign of Hotspur's militaristic prowess that in 1402 he was also appointed Royal Lieutenant in North Wales, tasked with bringing Glyndŵr to heel in a conflict that was quickly beginning to resemble nothing less than a Welsh war of independence.

Behind the scenes however, as the fighting intensified (the king was also fighting the Scots during 1402), Hotspur and the Percy family were growing increasingly dissatisfied with the realities of the new king's patronage. There was a long list of grievances building, chief among them, the king's failure to pay wages owed for the defence of the Anglo-Scottish border whilst also demanding that the Percys' hand over their Scottish prisoners; prisoners who would have traditionally found themselves ransomed in place of the missing wages.

Activities in Wales too brought their share of issues. Not only had the king failed to acknowledge a peace deal that had been drawn up courtesy of the Percys' hard and risky work, but the king had also then refused to pay a ransom for Hotspur's brother-in-law, Sir Edmund Mortimer, who himself had been captured by the Welsh. The Percy family, who had been promised so much, had come to take these repeated failures as personal slights. This was a serious, treacherous time in England, and it was vital that should a powerful family wish to survive, they must stay ahead of any portents and omens that were spotted in the skies above them.

The new king, whom they had helped to power, had seemingly proved himself less than loyal. And so, now allying with Glyndŵr's forces in Wales, the Percys opted to lead a fresh, open rebellion. Spearheaded by Hotspur himself, in the summer of 1403 the family mustered their regional connections and began a march south. Several high-ranking figures had rallied to join their retinue, all similarly slighted by the king and equally keen for redress, but it wasn't until they reached Cheshire that their forces would finally take the shape of a solid, operational concern.

Cheshire however, had recently seen troubles of its own, with an event we would do well to try and understand before placing Shipbrook into the greater fray. Just three years earlier, in March 1400, the Cheshire Rolls record that the Prince of Wales (and future King Henry V) has issued an order that all governors of Cheshire castles should take personal custody of their fortresses 'having consideration to the rebellions commenced by some of the county'. It is a reference to one of those events in Cheshire history that seems to have slipped through the cracks of the broader historical record, yet one intrinsically connected to the wider concerns of the nation at the time.

As a 'palatinate county' Cheshire was not subjected to the standardised laws of government with quite the same verve as many other counties. Rather, many of its judicious and administrative facets were influenced by auspices of direct Royal overture. It was our county, perhaps more than any other, that enjoyed a genuinely 'special relationship' with the Royal household during the period, particularly that of Richard II. Indeed, it was the company of soldiers known as the Cheshire Guard that had formed the personal bodyguard of the deposed King Richard II; and it was in the city of Chester that a force had gathered in 1399 in an attempt to drum up fresh support for his restoration.

Richard had been a genuine friend of the county and the concerns of its nobility, and for the most part, the Cheshire elite had little love for the incoming Henry.

Even when Henry was settled on his new throne, events of 1399 would not be easily forgotten, as there is a further mention in the record of more than 100 people in Cheshire being refused pardon in May 1400 due to 'treasons, insurrections, felonies, rebellions, and trespasses committed by them from Christmas last' - an apparent nod to Cheshire's distinctly Ricardian allegiances.

The interesting thing about this entry is that whilst such conflicts meant official pardons and the like were standard practice - how else could you crack on with running your new country if you refused to forgive those that had supported your predecessor - the new king specifically wanted personal apologies from those individuals concerned. He was a man clearly still much concerned about the rumination of their collective mindset.

The Manor of Shipbrook, there should be little doubt, would have been a major benefactor of the favourable esteem in which the deposed king had held his distant and loyal county. Still home to the Vernons, national events would have been watched with avid interest as the summer of 1403 began to unfurl with Hotspur making his way to Cheshire in search of support. Upon arrival, he would not be disappointed.

Irrespective of how personal the slights may have been at the heart of the Percy family rebellion, here was a chance for the nobility of Cheshire to call their houses together, enabling tangible action to manifest from the thick air of resentment that had been hanging around their great manors for the past four years; and with Hotspur at the head of the mission, it was recognised as being a cause with a genuine shot at success. Cheshire contained a wealth of experienced soldiers including the famed and feared Cheshire Bowmen, some of which were part of the aforementioned Cheshire Guard. Altogether, an estimated 10,000 souls would join the campaign as its rally passed through the county; and chief amongst them was Sir Richard Vernon of Shipbrook Castle.

The Battle of Shrewsbury

Hotspur would meet his new Cheshire army at Sandiway near Northwich, before marching to Whitchurch and then on again into deepest Shropshire. With Welsh reinforcements set to join them on route courtesy of Glyndŵr, the swollen throng of the Hotspur army moved south intending to take on the forces of both King Henry and the Prince of Wales in a single, definitive pitched battle.

Come the evening of the 20th of July, the Percys, together

with Sir Richard Vernon, got what they were looking for.

Upon reaching Shrewsbury and setting up camp on opposing banks of the Severn River, 30,000 fighters found themselves staring at one another across the water, banners blowing in the evening breeze. They retreated to their respective camps for the night, but as morning broke King Henry rounded a number of his troops and sent them north in a bid to cut off the rebel road back towards Chester. It didn't work, but in the attempt, he had shifted the would-be location of the battlefield toward the open ground of the village of Harlescott. With no river to divide them and the heat of the day rising, the fuse was lit.

The two sides lined up and began their parley, trading insults and war cries across the pea field. The king, as was the custom, and in a bid to avoid mass bloodshed, first offered terms for Hotspur's surrender. They were duly refused and as noon approached, the two sides began their advance. It was the first time in history that English bowmen had faced one another in combat, and it was with the archers that, late in the afternoon, the battle finally began.

The toll of the bowmen across both armies was great, but the Cheshire archers had superior skill, with the English chronicler Thomas Walsingham noting how the men of the king's army 'fell like leaves in Autumn, as every arrow struck a mortal man'. The Earl of Stafford, commanding the king's right flank, was killed in the onslaught and his forces, in disarray, fled the field leaving around 7000 horses behind. In the same hail of arrows that had taken Stafford's life, the Prince of Wales was himself hit with an arrow to the face, but he fought on regardless. A young man in the thick of the action, it was a bloodying that would stay with him throughout his life; later, as King Henry V, he would himself employ the Cheshire Bowmen on the field at the Battle of Agincourt.

In the madness of the fighting, with the rebels in the ascendancy, Hotspur had waited patiently, deliberately choosing his moment to strike. Charging directly at the king, Percy and his men crashed into the Royal ranks, the quartered-lion standard falling to the ground. Percy, lifting the visor on his helmet to assess the situation was then struck by an arrow. His men, seeing the fallen standard, exclaimed that the king was dead, but they soon found out he was not, as Henry lifted himself from the melee and declared that in fact it was Percy that was no more.

The battle was over, and the Percy family, together with their Cheshire supporters, were defeated. Hotspur's body would be salted before being impaled on a spear in Shrewsbury's marketplace. Then, being quartered, his torso was sent for display at Chester, and his head sent to York. It would be four months until his remains were finally returned to his widow.

Sir Richard Vernon would have been a significant player on the day of the battle, but perhaps even more so during the build-up. His influence from Shipbrook would have played a key part in organising the Cheshire force; something that illustrates just how important his seat had become. From contemporary records, and in particular the chronicle from Dieulacres Abbey in Staffordshire, we can learn a little more about Vernon's place in the uprising.

Along with Sir Edward Fitton of Gawsworth Hall, Vernon had served in the Irish campaigns of Richard II during 1399 and it would appear from the chronicle that Vernon, together with Sir Richard Venables of Kinderton, were the two most prominent figures of the Northwich hundred in the gathering storm of 1403. Both men were known to have received life-long pensions from Richard, and it was Vernon himself who had been appointed Commissioner for the Peace in Nantwich just a week before Richard lost his throne.

Just how influential a figure Sir Richard Vernon become during the rebellion is further illustrated by his inclusion in Shakespeare's play *Henry IV*. Shakespeare's plays are often thought to have been heavily influenced by political propaganda of the day, which is understandable, but increasingly, as with the case of Richard III, his depictions are becoming considered surprisingly accurate. In *Henry IV*, we get a portrait of Sir Richard Vernon as a man who often finds Hotspur's decisions at odds with his own better judgement. It is Vernon who is charged with informing Hotspur that the expected reinforcements under Owain Glyndŵr have failed to materialise (true to life) and we could perhaps take this as a nod to Vernon's genuinely elevated position in Hotspur's chain of command.

Despite his evident nobility, in defeat, it would follow that Vernon's contribution to the Percy cause be addressed as a matter of treason. With his men melting into the country night as they began their long and desperate journey back toward Cheshire, he was duly taken prisoner alongside Hotspur's uncle Thomas Percy and sent directly to Shrewsbury Gaol. There, he would be hanged, drawn, and quartered, before his head was spiked atop the city walls.

For Cheshire as a whole, the failure of the rebellion equated to a complete disaster, the dead on the field that night in Shrewsbury reading like roll-call of the county's great historic families. As a result, Cheshire would play little part in the later uprisings during Henry's reign. Safe to say, for Shipbrook Castle and the community that had come to rely on it, a difficult and troublesome time lay ahead. With Sir Richard Vernon's childless execution, Shipbrook Castle was cast into an inevitable quicklime.

The last of the Shipbrook Vernons arrive on the scene in the immediate aftermath of Shrewsbury, with Sir James Vernon of Lostock and Haslington. Upon inheriting the

Manor of Shipbrook in 1404, his family already more than comfortable with life at Haslington Hall some 12 miles to the south, it was the beginning of the end for life at the castle and it is shortly after the handover to James that the castle at Shipbrook slips away from the historical record altogether.

A Lost Heritage

The story of Shipbrook Castle is one that lasts for the better part of three hundred and fifty years. From its origin as a look-out over the River Dane, through its function as a Baronial seat of Royal influence and on to its decline following Sir Richard Vernon's gruesome end in 1403, Shipbrook and its custodians played a pivotal role in not only the development of Cheshire as we know it, but of England as a nation.

As mentioned earlier in this piece, stone remnants of the castle were reportedly still on site as late as 1790, when their last scraps were cleared away by a tenant - a Mr. Edward Tomkinson in the antiquarian record - in order to be used in the local farm buildings. Long-weathered, three stone lintels could still be spotted in a barn at the site as recently as the 1950s.

Today, the castle's former site is occupied by Shipbrook Hill Farm and the lovely Riverside Organic Cafe, where during summer months, families will take their children to sit above the riverbank, remark at the grazing livestock and enjoy ice cream from the local dairy. Whilst there, they will cast their eyes out across the Dane, over the river crossing, and on toward the pastures of Davenham; few realising just how much their experience connects with the very same line of thinking that made the site the chosen Baronial home of the de Vernon's almost 1000 years before.

For more than a brief moment on that summer afternoon in July 1403, it looked very much as though Hotspur and his Cheshire troops were going to emerge victorious. Had the Battle of Shrewsbury turned out differently, and Sir Richard Vernon's direct line survived as a result, it is entirely probable that the ruins of Shipbrook Castle would still stand today in a form that we would associate with that romantic image of the ruined English castle.

There would have been more trials for the building and the family who inhabited it, no doubt, and had it indeed survived the wars of the fifteenth century, who knows what fates would have befallen it come the English Civil War 240 years later. Yet if it had endured, I have little doubt that its crumbling walls would provide a degree of well-deserved recognition for an unassuming and picturesque corner of Cheshire that, at its heart, contains is a treasure trove of fascinating local history.

Scholar of Magic

Ranulf Higden and the Wands of Chester Cathedral

The Cheshire monk Ranulf Higden is remembered to historians today as the author of a distant world history from the fourteenth century. However, beyond his daily religious work in the abbey at Chester, he was an inquisitive and curious man of his age; traits that can help us understand better why such a figure of Christian piety would come to be buried with a notorious totem of the magical arts.

Break On Through

Renovations in historic buildings rarely pass without curious incident. Alongside the practical implications of removing stonework, altering floor levels, and repositioning artefacts, there is also a basic reality to be considered at every turn. There is a chance, no matter the intention, that those carrying out the work may come across human remains. It is simply unavoidable, and on occasion, sometimes those remains may be more famous than others.

There are few more explosive figures in English history than that of King Charles I. The man divided a country, led it into Civil War, and as a result of his subsequent beheading, inspired hundreds of pub names the length and breadth of the country. Following that execution in January 1649, where he reportedly wore two shirts to ensure his tremble in the winter air would not be taken for fear of his fate, his body was placed in a coffin and taken to the Chapel of St George in Windsor. A hundred years later though, there was no sign of his final resting place in Windsor. Somehow, nobody could quite remember where it was supposed to be, and rumours circulated that he had in fact been interred at Westminster Abbey, in secret, at the behest of his son King Charles II, sometime in the 1660s.

However, in the early 1800s, when a mausoleum was being built at Windsor under the personal instruction of King George III, workmen accidentally crashed through the wall of a passageway and into a vault containing the remains of King Henry VIII and his third wife, Jane Seymour. Dean of Windsor, Benjamin Charles Stevenson, was charged with making his way down into the vault to inspect the damage, where he was surprised to see a third coffin alongside those of Henry and Jane. The coffin was draped in a black velvet shroud and Stevenson knew his history. He recognised from the descriptions he had read that this could well be the missing coffin of King Charles I. Temptation soon overcame any notions of good taste.

Upon removing the shroud, the inscription was clearly visible. It was the coffin of the lost king, but it wasn't enough to simply recognise the fact, and so in the spirit of the human fascination with the macabre, he ordered the coffin open. Removing the covering from the head, he saw that the long face with a sculptured, pointed beard, bore a striking resemblance to that which had come to adorn all manner of coins, busts, and portraits of the late king. Yet still, confirmation of the face wasn't enough. And so, Stevenson lifted aloft the skull in the dim light of the chamber to check that it had indeed been separated from the body in accordance with a formal beheading.

I have to say, this conjures an image I find as equally

fascinating as I do gruesome, but it is a discovery that pales in comparison compared with the fascination we might find in our own forthcoming tale, as sometimes, the things we find in coffins hidden away in our most ancient buildings will raise far more questions than they could ever hope to answer. Sometimes, they compel and mystify, and an incident at Chester Cathedral during renovations there in the 1870s would certainly do just that, placing the very nature of the institution's Christian heritage into a rabbit hole of esoteric possibilities.

Founded in 1093 as the Benedictine Abbey of St. Werburgh, by the nineteenth century this county's grandest of structures was badly in need of repair. It had been at least 200 years since the last major conservation work had taken place and significant portions of the cathedral were now on the verge of collapse. Sandstone, for all its qualities, finds few friends in the elements hundreds of years from its initial setting, and various work projects would take place between 1820 and 1876 in an attempt to save the building for the future. It was during the later stages of this revival, under the auspices of the great Gothic architect George Gilbert Scott, that a find was made which gave cause for serious disquiet in local society circles.

Buried in the Cathedral were - and still are - a plethora of historical figures from Cheshire's past. These include Hugh d'Avranches, the 1st Earl of Chester, and Ranulf de Blondeville, the 6th Earl, and a veritable megastar of the High Middle Ages. One figure not quite as well known though was the fourteenth century chronicler and Benedictine monk, Ranulf Higden. It was when realigning his tomb, that by accident or design, his stone coffin was split open. Inside, Hidgen's remains were wrapped in the remnants of his burial shroud as expected, but atop it, perfectly preserved, was placed a long, hazel wand. A sign of pagan belief, curiosity and concern - in equal measure - soon began to smoulder in the conversations echoing throughout the cloisters of the cathedral.

To the Victorian mind, in an era enthused with the esoteric, the wand was quickly noted to be a tool of the occult, and so a natural question was posed as to just what business did such apparatus have being found in the sanctuary of a millennium-old centre of Christianity? It is a question that is yet to be answered, but one we will now dare to satisfy here.

Established under Roman rule as a major administrative centre, the city of Chester, or Deva to give it its Roman name, had been founded in 79 BCE by Emperor Vespasian and, if recently suggested theories are correct, it had likely been intended as the new capital of Britannia. This is something which would account for the fact that its amphitheatre, that traditional centre for gladiatorial and sporting games, is the largest of its kind in the whole of Britain, seating around 10,000 people. Its original fortress too was the largest in the province. The city was surrounded by plenty of navigable water and was located deep enough into the new Roman territory to suggest a natural command centre for the wider world around it. For a little while at least, it is hard to argue against Deva being viewed as one of the most important settlements in the whole of the Roman Empire.

With this firm foundation from Rome, naturally, the soldiers that found themselves at Deva - together with their families and dependents - would worship the plethora of Roman gods and goddesses that was their will throughout a tenure in the North West that lasted for more than three hundred years. When Rome officially withdrew from Britain in the year 410, the city would then be inhabited by a Romano-British people that had developed in the shadow of its imperial safety, continuing to utilise its fortress in order to provide sanctuary against the frequent raiding parties that would come in from Wales and Ireland. They would live with a history of its Roman heyday for hundreds of years; as late as the ninth century, Chester is still referred to as *Cair Legion* or the 'City of the Legion'.

As Roman rule gave way to the age of Scandi-Saxon conflict which followed, Chester surfaces on the record at various points denoting its continuing cultural and administrative importance. In 616 there comes the Battle of Chester, in which Æthelfrith of Northumbria defeats an invading Welsh force. A key event surrounding the battle was a massacre of monks from Bangor, who had been targeted for fear that they had been praying for the defeat of the Anglo-Saxon forces; a signpost to the emerging cult of Celtic Christianity that was beginning to rival the pagan belief system of the post-Roman world.

Seventy years later, Æthelred of Mercia would found a new church in the city. This church would grow, and Chester's Christian status would become cemented with it. By the tenth century, when the body of St. Werburgh, niece of the aforementioned Æthelred, was brought into the city in an attempt to ensure it was not violated during Norse raids in nearby Staffordshire, Chester had become a major religious centre at the heart of Saxon christendom. It was a sign of the city's emergence as such a centre that in 1093, following the destruction of the collegiate church, a new Benedictine Abbey was founded in its place, and it is in this building that we come to find Ranulf Higden living and working as a monk in the year 1299.

Scholar of Magic

It was a curious trait of the Benedictine order that, if a

member had a talent for writing, this would actively be encouraged to become their primary daily task, perhaps accounting for as much as six hours a day; virtually all the 'work' time available to the medieval monk outside of their religious rites and chores. It is something to which it seems Ranulf was particularly well suited and something that, should the curious mind choose to picture it, would give ample opportunity for all manner of literary investigations and conjectures to bear themselves out in the work of an inquisitive chronicler. It could even be considered just the kind of sympathetic situation required to guide a person with a curious mind towards less well-known pathways of thought.

Details as to his earlier life are as scant as you might imagine, but we do know that Ranulf Higden was born in or around the year 1280. Described by contemporary scholars as a 'man of the west country', by twenty years of age he had come to find himself in education at the Benedictine Abbey of St. Werburgh.

A monastic religious order within the Catholic Church, the Benedictines, or the 'Black Monks' in reference to the colour of their robes, were founded by Benedict of Nursia, an Italian monk who had become canonised due to his creation of a specific code for his fellow brothers to live by.

His canonisation was further helped by the fact that Benedict also knocked out an impressively diverse line in personal miracles, ranging from the practical (mending a piece of clothing by prayer) to the downright dangerous; Benedict once being credited with the exploding of a poisoned chalice - which had been handed to him by a group of nefarious monk - simply by looking at it. Growing out of the Italian peninsula during the sixth century, by the time of their Chester foundation, the order had come to be one of the most well-respected in all of Europe.

The life of a Benedictine was dominated by Benedict's 'Rule of Worship' - a series of daily rights stretching from 2 am until sundown. For most Benedictines however, aside from the devotion and work needed to run a successful monastery - 'to labor is to pray' being a favourite motto - there was also a real emphasis placed on the idea of learning; or more specifically, reading. Between prayer and its associated duties, at every spare moment, and even whilst eating their meals, there was a constant encouragement to read.

It was a part of Benedictine life that resonated at a volume within Higden. His talent for writing had been with him from an early age and is something that he would make a deliberate effort to nurture long into his adult life. In 1327, in his late forties, Ranulf drew on that lifetime of learning and skill as he compiled a work that would, for centuries to come, be considered the definitive work on the history of the known world; *Polychronicon*.

In so high esteem did this work place Higden that King Edward III himself would request his company in later life when in 1352 he was asked to visit the king at Westminster together with 'all your chronicles, and those which are in your charge to speak and take advice of'.

By the age, of 70, Ranulf Higden had become nothing less *the* bonafide authority on historical matters in England. His elevated status would have surprised few close to his field of study, the Polychronicon had been something of a sensation. Written in Latin, that first version of 1327 had been followed by further extended publications during the 1340s. Divided into seven books, as per the days of Genesis, it began with a geographical view of the world before going on to cover histories from Asia and Africa alongside that of Europe, with a substantial section devoted to the history of England from the period of the Saxons through to the reign of Edward III himself.

To this day, copies of Higden's final version of 1352 are held in esteemed libraries across the world, not least of all, in Vatican City.

There is a view that Higden had gleaned most of his knowledge from the works that surrounded him at the abbey, and whilst this would certainly be fitting of the times, and no doubt a great deal of study in-situ would have been necessary in order to create such a vast work as the Polychronicon was, there is also evidence to suggest he had gained certain aspects of his knowledge directly from his travels throughout the world surrounding him. This is particularly likely in respect of the subject matter that most of us would associate with the image of a wand like that with which Higden was buried; witchcraft. There is a direct reference within the Polychronicon to the witches of the western isles of Britain, and particularly the Isle of Mann, where we learn that;

> *In the Isle of Man is sorcery and witchcraft used, women*
> *there sell wind to the shipmen, closed under knots of thread,*
> *so that the wind he would have, the more knots he must undo.*

Western Isle witchcraft, with its distinctly elemental focus, had been known to scholars since at least the year 1200, with stories of how King Haakon of Norway had fallen victim to such forces on his visit to the region. A flood was reputedly raised by the witches of the West to blow clear his fleet for fear of their intent of invasion; the Isle of Mann being a province of Norway during until it came under Scottish rule in 1266. In a foreshadowing of King James' own work on the subject much later in 1597, the governor of the Isle of Man had written against using witchcraft as early as 1338.

My labour on this point is metered by the fact that Higden

is noted to have been a 'man of the West Country.' I wonder if there might not be some direct connection therefore with his knowledge of witchcraft in the Western Isles?

This connection is suggested directly from the contents of the Polychronicon itself, but it may well be that Higden had more localised knowledge on the subject too; having far more interaction with the world that existed beyond the confines of St. Werburgh's than has previously been considered. It is often overlooked, but the Polychronicon wasn't Higden's only published work. There was also *The Speciduiu Curatorum (Mirror for Priests)* and numerous others, specifically designed to be used by, and regarding the daily lives of, his fellow monks. What draws further interest for us, however, are the works he is *suspected* to have written, and those that may give us insight into another, more colloquial side of his character; namely, the *Chester Mystery Plays*

Local Fascinations

Mystery plays were popular across Europe from the thirteenth century right through to the middle of the 1700s. They primarily consisted of performances based on Bible stories, designed to spread the word of God to audiences that would otherwise struggle to perceive the messages within due to the Latin language barrier. In effect, it was the Bible, live on stage, for the masses. What could possibly go wrong?

Performed outside the church entrance, in the street, or at common markets, the Chester plays are one example of several well-preserved in England, with others associated with Coventry and York that are still relatively well understood today. First performed by the monks themselves and then also by members of local guilds too, the plays were the cause of some controversy in their heyday, as naturally, such public performance could easily - and often did - create something akin to a carnival atmosphere.

There would be ale drinking, feasting, and a whole parade of wagons filled with cavorting patrons. In Chester itself, a dedicated carnival route was established, moving along Northgate and Watergate before crossing to Bridge Street. The route would spark no less than three straight days of celebration on Witsun week in early summer, beginning in the morning and lasting long into the darkened hours. Quite the spectacle, the plays would eventually be banned in 1578 on account of their perceived ability to inspire debauchery in the common people of the city.

Higden is thought by many experts to have been the original writer of the Chester plays performed during the fourteenth century, and it is his association with them (as opposed to anything specifically included within) that should draw our curiosity now. A talented writer of his time undoubted, but his position in relation to the creation of the mystery plays shows both a desire to mingle with the local population and an acute knowledge of its sensibilities. Not the kind of thing that you would expect from the reclusive character that Higden has long been stated to have been.

When held against his knowledge of the wind-knots of the Western Isles, we may well find a reason to inquire as to the likelihood of opportunity Higden may have had to enrol himself with the folk of the countryside at large, and therefore too, their practice of country witchcraft. And as we will now see, the issue of witchcraft itself was far from taboo for brothers of the Benedictine order in England during the period. If anything, it was nothing less than an officially sanctioned source of exploration.

Esoteric texts were part and parcel of the library for any Benedictine abbey. The order's focus on education and reading meant that there was a real cultural breadth to the material that their brethren would consume, but thanks to the catalogue of one location in particular during the period - the Benedictine abbey of St. Augustine's in Canterbury - we can get a real sense of just how deep that exploration ran, in the vein of specifically denoted 'magical' books.

More than thirty such texts were donated to St Augustine's across the medieval period, helping to form a collection of works that actively promoted ideas associated with the magical arts. Part of the logic for this was that in the working of Christian prayer, a certain kind of supernatural force was deemed to have already been at play. Naturally, this meant that anything mimicking a similar act would form a legitimate field of study, be it to prove or disprove anything that did or did not align with accepted Christian doctrine.

There is evidence from the same period as Higden's life, set out wonderfully in Sophie Page's *Magic in the Cloister* from 2013 (an extraordinary academic work on the topic) that the monks investigating such matters were far from adverse to attempting certain charms and spells themselves, most pointedly with the aim of bettering the order's lot economically. Mostly written in Latin, but sometimes of Arabic influence too, the idea of metaphysical magic was a popular subject for those living and working in closed abbey communities. It was, ironically given the backlash on such subjects that would come later in the early modern period, viewed as a legitimate gateway to spiritual knowledge.

Partaking in the practical application of such spells and charms was often justified with philosophical arguments and rationale centred around a combative mindset that was growing through an age of increasing scientific revisionism. Even when such texts should have proven controversial, the fact that many survive today shows the level of toleration afforded to the subject. At St Augustine's, the monks involved in the collating of magical texts were never accused of anything other than diligent hard work, and it is that collection, still intact come the dissolution of 1538, that would ultimately end up in the private collection of that most infamous of sixteenth century polymaths, Dr. John Dee. The fact is, the very order of which Higden was a brother was the primary safe-house of magical learning in the whole of medieval Christendom.

Hazel Lore

Having established that the idea of a Benedictine monk being somehow connected to the matter of practical magic in the medieval period as being far from outlandish, we should now look to the ideas centred on the issue of the hazel wand itself. In British folklore, which so often provides the best hope of understanding when dealing with such distant, obscured practices, hazel is often associated with the warding away of evil spirits. More broadly, however, as we stretch across varied cultures, the primary association for hazel is that as a symbol of knowledge.

Relatively commonplace in the grave pits of European prehistoric burials and too in Eastern mythology, far from denoting an active practitioner of magic per-se, hazel wands have long been associated with protection *against* witchcraft. Rather than a tool of the wielder, they are the rebuttal and the shield.

Whilst the motivations which lay behind the full meaning of such an object being placed in the tomb of Ranulf Higden may be eternally lost to us, the isolated fact that it was placed there at all can offer us a real window into its wider cultural context. Quite obviously, Ranulf did not place the wand there himself, meaning that its relevance and suitability for Higden in death must have been known by others at the time. That is to say, someone else, and most likely a figure of influence, thought it appropriate. Perhaps even necessary. That other party too would have been part of the Benedictine order in Chester come Ranulf's death on 12th March 1364; an observation which glows hot with possibilities for the imagination when we learn that incredibly, Ranulf's burial was not the only one at the abbey to be marked with the placement of such a wand.

When it comes to such burial rites being carried out in the cathedral at Chester, I am drawn to entries made in the local press at the time of the discovery of Higden's wand. A magazine for curious gentlemen, where those so minded could find a forum to write with questions and replies in each issue, *The Cheshire Sheaf* of May 1878 reads that;

> *Some three or four years ago, when the grave of Ranulf Higden, the historian, was discovered in Chester Cathedral, it was stated that in that and another tomb in an adjoining aisle there had been found a long hazel stick placed, in each case, across the sere-clothed body. There must have been some significance, occult or otherwise, in this curious burial customer, and I should be pleased to learn any information you may pick up for me therefore. G.T*

G.T are the given initials of the question's poser, and in reply, we have this from the equally mysterious T.T;

> *The Hazel stick found in the two ancient tombs in Chester cathedral named by G.T, as also in a similar grave of Abbot Birchylles in the Lady Chapel there, many years before, shows the prevalence of superstition amongst people in high places in the earlier days of the English Church. Its use, under such circumstances, was held to be an antidote against witchcraft and all other evils in the future of the deceased. I am aware that the wand so placed in the grace has been regarded by some antiquaries as a badge of authority, and I know that the bishop's pastoral staff or the abbot's crook is not infrequently so found, but I can see no reason why a mere roughly-cut*

switch of the hazel tree should be regarded as a religious symbol. My belief is that blind superstition was at the bottom of it all. T.T

Abbot Birchells is recorded as being at the abbey during the 1320s, a time when Higden was deep into the writing of the Polychronicon, and an abbot noted in chronicles of the time for holding 'too many feasts', eating meat on fish days and using the abbeys funds to buy up books for his personal use. There was also a scolding noted, recording how under Abbot Birchells some monks had started to dress differently in an apparent attempt to denote their status. That the abbot heading the abbey during Higden's heyday should too come to be buried with a hazel wand is quite the point of note. Far from being an outlying curiosity of abbey life in Chester during the fourteenth century, it may be evidence that this cult of the wand was relatively well established, even to the point of being enshrined in the burial of the abbot himself.

Natural Wonders

Ranulf Higden was a remarkable scholar of the fourteenth century whose chief work would be held in esteem by the broader church for more than 200 years. Besides this remarkable feat of medieval academia, we also have good cause to believe him a man of studious local interest, in both the people and places of Cheshire and further afield too. His place at the heart of the Chester Mystery Plays may be speculative from an empirical historian's view, but is well in keeping with the comparatively fun-loving attitude of his head abbot when we consider the feasts and revelry apparently so favoured by the man in charge.

In a Benedictine order known to have journeyed extensively within occultist realms, clear to us courtesy of their magical collections down in Canterbury, that both men should be buried with a totem of magical working and protection, calls out to a greater creation around them; a belief system entwined with, yet notably distinct from, the clearly defined ordained structure for which their order would outwardly be known throughout Europe. Commemoration in death, and the objects we are buried with, is perhaps the greatest testament to our personal beliefs that it is possible to share, all the more so during eras of the past.

The idea of Higden as some kind of Cheshire warlock is admittedly quite fantastical, but the image of Higden purely as an ecclesiastical historical scholar doesn't quite fit the evidence left to us either. In his story, we find a gateway toward the paradoxical realities of religious life during the fourteenth century. The mystics of rural society were, both during Higden's time and long after, something to which the Church publicly cast a troubled eye whilst the other looked toward them with marked curiosity. The broader hinterland of study in which their beliefs were recorded, that of magical texts, formed a core knowledge base free from taboo. Once we remove our more modern assumptions, there is no hint of secretive, guilty pleasure to be fostered onto the subject at all.

The reading and understanding of such works would have provided a perfectly legitimate endeavour within the structure of the order, encouraged, intending to ensure that no hidden gem of God's own law was unfurled by the less pious. If anything, it was a clear case of it being a necessity to 'know your enemy', and if that enemy was the Devil, his strategies and techniques were thought to be naturally abundant in the work of witchcraft. Of course, such time spent on the topic, alone in the candle-lit rooms of the abbey, was bound to create a more personal interest too.

It was a relationship in which the brethren were directly in contact with the enticements such subjects could illicit for the reader. That such a connection was made seems apparent by the evidence of the burial rites of both Higden and Birchells, but it is only our modern interpretation, or perhaps more accurately our tether to the long lingering ideas of the Victorian age, which grant a sense of mischief to the whole affair.

It is far more likely that Higden was just as fascinated by the idea of magic as we are today, and that for a brief moment, the bonding of Christianity and witchcraft was metered out in the actions of certain members of the Benedictine order in Cheshire. After all, when we consider it, when it comes to magical acts, the two may be considered inherently connected.

I mean, just how does someone turn water into wine? Or for that matter, feed 5,000 people with just five loaves of bread and two small fish? For the religious scholars of his age, an inquisitive study of magical possibilities may well have been the very thing expected of great academic minds such as that possessed by Brother Ranulf Higden. What he came to understand through his work, symbolised for eternity by the hazel wand placed carefully in his tomb.

The Last Day of August

Great Budworth's Civil War Secret

The village of Great Budworth possesses one of the most remarkable churches in all of Cheshire, not just loved by locals but genuinely appreciated by history fans and enthusiasts of late medieval architecture right across the UK. Something they may not be aware of however is the visit paid to the village by Parliamentarian forces on the last day of August in 1644 and its place at the centre of a genuinely hidden history of the English Civil War.

Signs of War

For many of us with an active interest in local history, a passion for local churches is a healthy and seriously rewarding sideline to develop. Beyond its obvious role as a religious house and focal point for the local community, the parish church is also a bastion of historical insight. In the absence of a castle (and sometimes even still) the parish church will likely be the oldest building to be found in our village or town, and as such it has found itself playing the primary witness to, and chronicler thereof, hundreds and sometimes thousands of years of local life. In this guise it will naturally find itself performing another role too; as a keeper of secrets.

From the shape of the tower or the main doorway, a visitor may deduce the origins of a more ancient building with relative ease. A round tower, originally defensive, likely made from knapped flint, is almost always a rare reminder of our Saxon heritage. An original Norman church will have a squared tower, and a semi-circular archway, often decorated with zig-zag or chevron shapes around the door. There are clues everywhere as to the age of the building, even in the buttresses of the walls; Norman structures tend to be flat and broad, and early English from circa 1200 projecting slightly with a slopped cap, with later styles tending to be free-standing, joining the wall by way of an arch. So much information and that's without even beginning to consider window styles and general stonework.

In the churchyard too, with its features and tracks, the visitor may be able to learn more about the historical setting of the village surrounding the church. Is the churchyard raised above the level of the church floor? If so, by how much? The average English parish church has seen upwards of ten thousand burials over the past eight hundred years, which is why so many of them now present as elevated (try not to think about that too much next time you're walking through one at night).

Courtesy of the various pamphlets, effigies, and mounted plaques to be found in a church of antiquity, going inside the building you may find that understanding can be gained as to the key players in the life of the building and area, be them local nobles or wealthy landowners. Look closer still and there may even be antiquated graffiti on the walls, not to mention the daisy-wheel hexafoil, 'W' and 'X' symbols that may be found around its doors and windows; 'witch-marks' from a time when local communities genuinely believed that evil spirits could be deterred from crossing a threshold by such carvings in the stone. As you may well be able to tell, some of us can get a tad obsessive about this stuff!

Now for most, any selection of these discoveries will quite rightly provide more than an ample return for a day's historical enquiry. However, as one of the few stone constructions in the vicinity of the village, and of course the only place with a tower to provide a lookout, the parish church has also become acquainted with, an often under-appreciated timeline of local history too; war.

From the Baronial conflicts of the Middle Ages, through the events of the Wars of the Roses, and onto the English Civil Wars of the mid-seventeenth century, the parish church has repeatedly come to find itself at the centre of a militarised experience. Occasionally, these chapters in its history will be known in the local area, but for the most part, it is left to the researchers and amateur historians to piece together the puzzles hidden, not only in the dusty recesses of the local historical record but often too in the very fabric of the building itself.

They may go unreferenced in the guidebook, but look more closely at the stonework inside the church and you may well spot deep score marks left from idle hours of billeted troops that found themselves with little to do but sharpen their weapons in readiness for battle. Then outside the church, around the doors, windows, and towers, we may come across what I often consider to be the jewel of such studies; circular depressions made from musket fire. It was the unexpected observation of such that inspired this piece, for whilst many of the topics I cover centre on reappraising age-old legend and folklore, this one came about through my own personal experience back in the summer of 2021, as a summer stroll in a churchyard led me to uncover the details of a long since obscured Civil War shoot-out in the heart of the Cheshire countryside.

A Beautiful Village

The village of Great Budworth sits in the upper eastern quadrant of Cheshire, surrounded by rolling, untouched countryside, and makes for a perfect example of the classic English village of yore. It is a place with a deep-rooted history, its name coming from the Saxon words *bode* and *wurth*, meaning 'a dwelling by water' in reference to its proximity to the nearby mere. Noted in *Domesday Book* as already having a resident priest back in 1086, it would go to spend much of its history as part of the Arley Hall estate, right up until 1948; something which did much to preserve the look and feel of the village so admired today.

Popular with location scouts and TV crews, its cobbled lanes and cottages offer the visitor a rare and tangible route back into the past. A route that, at every turn, finds itself in the shadow of the wonderful fourteenth century church of St. Marys and All Saints. A building described in *Buildings of England*, a foremost book on English architecture, as one of the finest examples of ecclesiastical architecture remaining in Cheshire, not only is the church a historical gem, but the church grounds also play home to the former village school; a remarkably well-persevered timber-framed building built back in 1615.

A tour of the church itself brings with it many delights, not least the effigy of Sir John Warburton of Arley Hall, replete in full dress armour. However, it was the stunning fifteenth century octagonal font that caught my attention most when I visited that summer day on account of a sign noting its re-discovery in 1868 - having been hidden under the church floor during the English Civil War. There was nothing in the guidebooks regarding the church's connection to the conflict, yet this was obviously a serious moment in the history of the village. Such absence of commentary is not unusual.

The fallout of such civil conflicts was often highly political, and in times gone by that meant highly dangerous too. The need to side with the victors, to ensure safety, often saw locals needing to simply get on with life under the new regime, religious or otherwise, as quickly and quietly as possible. As such, the details of the associated conflict often became taboo for those immediately connected to the church.

The Civil War had played out in various spots across Cheshire, and several churches in the county make passing comment about it on their websites and in their guides. Most locally to Great Budworth, Tarvin Church, around 16 miles to the south-east, is a particular favourite of mine in this regard, displaying as it does dozens of musket shot holes around its tower and west wall, the scars of a skirmish that took place in the village during the August of 1644.

The news that Great Budworth had been so affected by the war, for surely the requirement to hide a solid stone font beneath the church floor was a concession to precisely that fact, was, however, something of an unknown quantity to me. Armed with this new information, I took it upon myself to examine the church exterior a little more closely. It would lead to the most enthralling experience I have ever had while exploring such a location, stoking my imagination and passion for the topic ever since.

Where contemporary buildings are found in close proximity to a church that was present during the Civil War, it is not uncommon to discover evidence of a firefight; marks left from the muskets of Royalists and Parliamentarian troops firing over close distances, closing in on one another as one side seeks to overthrow the other from what is primarily a valuable strategic position. At

Great Budworth, many of the surrounding houses are likely contemporary but better than that, the schoolhouse of 1615, as mentioned previously, is located on the church grounds. I had missed it at first, but sure enough, as I looked again, shot marks, more in keeping with a Flintlock pistol than a musket (such pistols are known to have been in wide use during the conflict, especially by members of the cavalry) were scattered around the schoolhouse door. And then I saw it. A very deliberate 'R' etched into the stonework.

It was one of those rarest of moments, a mainline straight into the past, at least it would be, if it was, as I suspected, etched in reference to Royalist allegiance. Turning 180 degrees to work out the angle of the gunfire trajectory, I then found what looked suspiciously like corresponding shot marks in the corner space of the walls between the vestry and the Lady Chapel. Was this the material memory of a shoot-out? It was easy to see how the corner space would provide cover for a soldier firing onto someone doing similar from the doorway of the school. What happened here? I was relishing the challenge of trying to find out.

Civil War Cheshire

The Civil War in Cheshire is, as you might expect, a

complex history that contains as many rabbit holes of exception and contradiction as it does anything like clear lines. Following the king raising his standard at Nottingham in 1642, and the promise of Parliament's response, for most local communities during the first year of the war, the focus was entirely centred on attempting to preserve a state of neutrality. In the beginning, it was more about ensuring the safety of your local resources than any rallying cries, with local militias setting out to avoid involvement in militarised political conflict and simply protect their families. Come 1643 however, the sheer breadth of the war meant this was no longer possible, and some relatively well-defined divisions of support had been carved out.

For the majority of the war to come, the west of the county, and the city of Chester in particular, would be cast as bastions of the Royalist cause. Provisioned and defended - and visited by King Charles in person twice - the Cheshire region acted as a buffer between Parliamentarian England and the Royalist loyalists of North Wales. Central and eastern Cheshire however would soon find themselves largely under Parliamentary control, with the Parliamentarian headquarters for the region set up in Nantwich - Sir William Brereton of Handforth Hall taking on the role of regional commander.

Most key conflicts in the county took place early in the war, with Brereton moving quickly to take key towns during

1643, with notable battles at Middlewich bookending the year. The war had brought brothers face to face on the battlefield in a very literal sense, dividing families and generations. This is a war let us not forget, that per head of the population, killed more in England and Wales than the First World War. By the winter of 1643, for everyone, the conflict had become a brutal, bloody, and totally unavoidable affair.

Yet no matter the perception of majority Parliamentarian control of the county that history has passed down to us, during that winter, Royalist designs on central Cheshire were still very much a going concern. In December, a force of some 3000 Royalist soldiers and 500 horses arrived in the Dee estuary from Ireland. When meeting up with Lord Byron's men from Oxford, who had recently surged into Cheshire taking back many towns and villages for the king, this new force meant a significant Royalist pack was available to be put to use in Cheshire for the first time since the outbreak of hostilities.

Spending several weeks at wild in the county, this local field army caused significant disruption to Parliamentarian plans, as Lord Byron managed to galvanise his men into a fighting unit that possessed much more bite than the local Parliamentarians had been used to. It was a detachment of this new force that attacked Beeston Castle, that great clifftop fortress of the thirteenth century perched atop

Beeston Crag that had been controlled by Brereton since 20th February. It was a highly prized strategic asset, as nothing much could happen for miles around without it being spotted by whoever commanded the position.

By winter, its crumbling walls had been repaired, its motte cleared, and it was now a very workable stronghold once more. The new force from Ireland however, in a band led by Captain Thomas Sandford, saw it as a prize ripe for the taking and one that, once captured, would send a defiant message to Parliamentarian soldiers located across the county. On December 13th, Sandford and his elite team infiltrated the castle's defences, scaling the cliff, and confronted the castle governor Captain Steele. So shocked was Steele at the covert attack, he surrendered on the spot. The Royalists would claim the castle for the king, and they wouldn't be turfed out again for the better part of two years; the siege that eventually dislodged them in November 1645, providing the basis for the destruction of the castle which resulted in the ruins we see today.

The taking of the Beeston illustrates well just how problematic a patchwork of allegiant colours was to be set beneath the veil for Cheshire during the year to come; a time filled by events that would ultimately send the blood-stained fingers of the war reaching for the village of Great Budworth.

1644

The year started with the Battle of Nantwich on 25th
January. At the time, following Byron's successful counter-
offensive before Christmas and his defeat of
Parliamentarian forces in Middlewich on December 26th,
Nantwich had briefly found itself as the only
Parliamentarian garrison in Cheshire.

Quartered in the snow around the village of Acton, it was
only a matter of time before Byron's new Cheshire army
would attempt to take Nantwich too. Its garrison was led
by a local noble, Colonel George Booth of Dunham
Massey, and although strategically vulnerable, was still
strong in fighting terms with around 2000 men at arms.
Bryon encircled the town on January 18th, knowing that
should he kick the garrison into touch, Cheshire would
officially become a Royalist county once more. What he
didn't know, however, was that additional Parliamentarian
forces were already on the way, led by the esteemed Sir
Thomas Fairfax, who was at that time in the war,
Commander in Chief of the whole Parliamentarian army.

On 24th January, Fairfax entered the region, his first
contact coming with a group of Royalist outriders that had
been sent to guard the road from Delamere Forest. Word
reached Byron, but he was none too concerned,
determined to focus on his siege of the town. The next

morning, however, as it so often does, nature intervened in the course of events.

A sudden thaw of the snow had seen the River Weaver rise dramatically, sweeping the beam-bridge away in its wake before Bryon had time to move his troops onto dryer ground. In the upshot, he was instead forced to move his men some 6 miles away to the bridge at Minshull Vernon so that he might maintain communication lines back to his camp at Acton, where his artillery was being stored in the churchyard.

The situation proved the perfect target for the advancing Fairfax. His forces engaged, outflanking the Royalist right, and immediately took the upper hand as Booth led 600 musketeers out of Nantwich to overrun the camp in Acton churchyard. By mid-afternoon, the battle was over, and more than 1500 of Byron's troops were taken prisoner, with Byron himself retreating to Chester. Never again in the course of the war would the Royalists have the chance to take back Cheshire for the king.

In the wider war, the spring of 1644 saw the Parliamentarians make gains across the country. The king's new capital at Oxford was now under serious threat and his northern stronghold of York was under siege. It is onto this stage that Prince Rupert of the Rhine, nephew of the king and the man from whom the atypical swashbuckling image of the Cavalier is thought to be drawn, found his calling. Initially intending to aid the Royalists in York, he had stormed the Parliamentarian garrison at Stockport before heading to Bolton, ordering an attack amidst heavy rain. Rupert's forces were repelled, with hundreds killed in the process, but he was undeterred, persisting with hand-to-hand fighting in the streets across the evening of 28th May until he finally won the day. It would be recorded as the Massacre of Bolton, as in the aftermath, Rupert's forces are reported to have slaughtered more than 1000 people in the town.

As the people of Cheshire waited to discover what tricks and trials may hit them next, in truth life for the most part became relatively settled across the summer months, and it is precisely because of this that the more unusual occurrences that did pipe up during the season are relatively well attested in the record; amongst which, we find our occasion at Great Budworth.

With Cheshire now back in Parliamentarian control, yet Chester itself being chock full of Royalist soldiers, it was only natural that one side should wish to keep a close eye on the other. For the Parliamentarians, this was a relatively easy task, with dedicated patrols on major highways and throughout the country green. For the Royalists in Chester however, with little to no information of events surrounding them making it through the lines, they needed to ride out and actually have a look for themselves. For the most part, this went unnoticed. When they did get caught though, things could get very ugly, very fast.

On Sunday 18th August, Colonel Marrow, a Royalist commander stationed in Chester, left the city with a small band of infantry and horse on advancement towards Northwich. It would have been a scouting exercise like any other, except that Marrow was something of a kleptomaniac when it came to livestock. He was renowned for it, and so on this trip, locals were keen to alert Parliamentarian soldiers in the area in an attempt to save their animals.

As Marrow's scout party reached Hartford Green near Davenham, they were duly met with a detachment of Parliamentarians who had arrived in an attempt to ward the Royalists off back towards Chester. A chase ensured, back out of the village, until a full fight broke out at the crossroads at Sandiway; details of which are left to us in a work that will prove invaluable to us in tracing the rest of our story.

Memorials of the Civil War in Cheshire and the Adjacent Counties, compiled by Edward Burghall, Vicar of Acton in 1899, is an incredible resource for the Civil War in Cheshire, as its original author, Thomas Melbon was keeper of the parish records at St Mary's Church in Acton - the churchyard used for the Royalist camp at the Battle of Nantwich - during the war, and so had an avid real-time interest, writing his account of the Civil War shortly after its end.

Regarding the fight at Sandiway, he writes;

> *Colonel Marrowe slane. On Sunday 18 Aug 1644*
> *Colonel Marrowe issued further of Chester with all or most*
> *of the horse & foote their, and marched towards Northwich;*
> *by the way, they plundered some poor men's cattle; but some of*
> *them, appearing onto the Townsmen on Hertford Green, had*
> *the forces in town issued upon them; which they perceiving, fled*
> *before towards Sandiway. The Townsmen pursued them, and*
> *the king's men took fifteen of them prisoners & carried them*
> *away; but Colonel Marrowe was shot in Sandiway by one*
> *lying under a hedge, & was carried alive into Chester, where*
> *he died the next day afterward.*

It was the aftermath of this confrontation from which several local events, long remembered from the conflict, take their genesis. Leaving Sandiway, a section of the Royalist force made for the village of Tarvin. We know this as just two days on, Parliamentarian forces from the garrison at Nantwich attacked Tarvin Church, where they took more than 40 prisoners and killed 15 soldiers in retaliation. Tarvin had been plagued by similar events since the outbreak of hostilities in Cheshire, and it is Tarvin's church, the twelfth century St. Andrew's, that I referred to earlier as exhibiting one of the 'best' examples of musket fire marking in the whole of England. The exterior walls are peppered. It is a fascinating sight and a grim reminder of events in the aftermath of the fight at Sandiway. I say that as although there were, as aforementioned, several other skirmishes in the town during the war, all others appear to have been raiding parties sent out by the Royalist garrison at Chester to attack Parliamentarian troops billeted in the village.

This instance is different, and the likely cause of the damage, as the only people that would need to take shelter in the church in a Parliamentarian village, and then be shot at - apparently lined up against the exterior wall - would be fleeing Royalist troops. It is what happened in the days that followed that is so important for us and the quest regarding events at Great Budworth.

Again, from troop movements attested to in *Memorials* we learn that on Friday 30th August, in light of the recent trouble at Tarvin, a large number of Parliamentarian troops - the whole of the Parliamentarian garrison from Nantwich - marched out to reinforce defences at Tarvin. However, having spent the night of the 30th at Middlewich, they then made a deliberate detour north to Great Budworth on the 31st.

Tarvin, as the crow flies, is around 15 miles east of Middlewich, so a journey to Great Budworth on-route means that the Parliamentarians were actively choosing to make a twenty-mile round trip, off-track from their desired destination.

Moving troops at the best of times was not a welcomed task. Mobilising a garrison, leaving their station unguarded but for the local militia, would never be something undertaken unless it was deemed absolutely necessary. For Tarvin, with aspirations as a market centre, one might understand the desire to reinforce and ensure the defences were up to speed, should the Royalists employ a sustained revenge attack. It would be seen as a worthwhile enterprise, and something to which such manpower - perhaps 500 strong - would add serious expediency. Therefore, for the detour, there was clearly something in Great Budworth, a village with a population of just a couple of hundred souls, that was of sufficient importance to draw the curiosity of an entire garrison force.

Royal Sympathy

The Warburton family of Arley Hall has a long history with Great Budworth, a key feature of St. Marys and All Saints Church is known as the Warburton Chapel and we know the village was officially part of the Arley estate until as recently as 1948. It is this connection to the Warburton family that was the likely reason for the Nantwich garrison visiting the village on August 31st, 1644.

History has come to view the Warburton family as fierce Royalists. Just how fierce is attested by the fact that John Warburton, born in 1587, was noted as being a 'Cavalier' at 60 years of age in local records. But it is his son William that was the major player in the conflict; and long after too. William would play a role in Sir George Booth's rebellion of 1659, in which the Battle of Winnington Bridge - a skirmish in Northwich that has been remembered as 'the last battle' of the English Civil Wars - featured as part of the uprising in support of the pending restoration of the monarchy following the removal of Oliver Cromwell's son Richard as head of the state.

Furthermore, an entry can be found in a collection called *The Works of the Right Reverend William Warburton*, published in 1788, that shows just how much of an impact William made on the Civil War, noting;

> *William Warburton distinguished himself in the Civil Wars... of the Royal party, showed his zeal and activity in that cause.*

We can somewhat safely assume therefore that such loyalties were firmly established at Arley during 1644, courtesy of the Warburton family, and so then too in Great Budworth - regardless of how sensitively local circumstance required them to be nourished. When we place this alongside the Parliamentarian need to detour to Great Budworth in the immediate aftermath of the fighting at Tarvin, it is likely due to the village being well known by Royalists as sympathetic to their plight, and in turn to the Parliamentarians as something of a niggling concern in the back of their minds.

It is entirely plausible then, or even likely, that in seeking refuge from the swarming Parliamentarian forces of August 1644, a detachment of Royalists deliberately made their way to the village in search of sanctuary. The issue of the font being hidden as it was - so hurriedly that it wouldn't be uncovered again for more than 200 years - is particularly telling in this regard.

Sympathetic villagers, all of which would be closely bound to - and reliant on - the Warburton family for their livelihood, would hurriedly look to hide away precious objects before the Parliamentarians arrived. This is a theory that is much more than conjecture. We know the Parliamentarian army visited that day, and we know that means they must have had a distinct reason to.

Maybe they were tipped off, or perhaps more likely still, it was an open secret that safe harbour for Royalists, no matter the colour of the county at large, could be found in the village of Great Budworth.

It is curious that the font was forgotten following the visit of the Roundheads; perhaps a further indicator as to the severity of the incursion. History is littered with stories of treasure, money, and important objects being buried by locals as soldiers advanced toward their village. Thing is, most of the time, the reason those things then become lost for hundreds of years, is that the people responsible for hiding them die in the resulting fight.

I am tempted to believe that there was no great number of Royalist soldiers in the village, as the suspected musket shot damage is comparatively small to that at Tarvin, but perhaps it was the case that a small group of soldiers had found cause to shelter in the schoolhouse when the forces from Nantwich arrived. Irrespective of the size of the Royalist cohort, it is clear that the Parliamentarian garrison had cause to suspect the group was dangerous enough to warrant the full force.

Arriving in the village, attention seems to have been drawn to both the church and the schoolhouse located in the churchyard. The distance between the two, and the stonework that would provide adequate cover, is no more than twenty meters. All of this is, of course, centred on the Royalist 'R' inscribed on the stonework beside the door of the schoolhouse built in 1615; an act which does much to fire the imagination. I am tempted to see the insignia as having been carved out as an act of defiance by those supporters of the king who were bunkered inside. It is way too much of a coincidence otherwise when we consider the events of the historical record.

The fate of those Royalists confronted that August day in Great Budworth is lost to us now, but three possibilities exist. They may have been killed, potentially along with those who had hidden the font, if this had indeed occurred at the same time and not earlier in the war. It may be the most dramatic conclusion, granted, but it is one worth considering given there is no record of prisoners being taken from the village at the time. That of course, is the second possible outcome; that those in the village, the quarry of the Nantwich garrison, were taken into custody. That said, the fate of those royal troops that had seemingly been executed against the wall at St. Andrew's in Tarvin might go some way to suggesting this was not the case.

If those at Great Budworth were aware of those darkly lit local events, it may well have been seen as all the more reason to make some kind of last stand in the churchyard. The third possibility, and the one that may challenge the first, is that no one was killed at all. That the etching of the 'R' predated the arrival of the Parliamentarian troops, and that it was left as one-in-the-eye for them upon arrival. It is something that fits well with the fact the event itself is almost entirely lost to history.

It would also fit a theory that, given the village's close-knit relationship with the Warburton family, anyone seeking shelter there would likely be tipped off about the Parliamentarian advances as they grew nearer to the village itself.

There would be further clashes between Royalists and Parliamentarians in Cheshire, both skirmishes and more pitched battles, mainly in 1645, when the king's men began their last great push in the county, again seeing armed action at Tarvin before a clash in Delamere Forrest saw the majority of the Royalist force killed or captured. The City of Chester, the last Royalist stronghold in the county and their last working deep-water port in the whole of England, would come under Parliamentarian artillery bombardment from 22 September, and on the 24th, King Charles himself would watch from the Phoenix Tower on the city walls as his armies were defeated at Rowton Moor.

It was a battle that, despite Chester itself holding out against the siege until February '66, brought an end to any sense of effective Royalist fighting forces in the county.

The war would rage on elsewhere, in ever-decreasing circles for the Royalist cause, their remaining cavalry force eradicated in an ambush at Sherburn-in-Elmet that October. Eventually, seeking support in his ancestral home nation of Scotland, Charles himself would be caught, and ultimately executed on January 30th, 1649. John Bradshaw, the man who was given the title of President of High Court of Justice for the king's trial, and chief amongst the signatories of his death warrant, was a Cheshire man himself, attending The King's School in Macclesfield and working as a clerk in Congleton before moving to London and far more lofty stations of life.

The English Civil War, or *Wars* as it is often now more accurately called, is a vast and complicated period of English history. No better is this shown than after all of the fighting, spilling of guts and ruined castle walls, and even after the king's head had rolled to a halt upon the scaffold at Whitechapel that cold winters day, it would be another ten years before the final battle - more of a skirmish in reality - would be fought. Ultimately, come 1659, despite Cromwell's role as Lord Protector and figurehead of the republic, the powers that be decided that amongst the political skullduggery that such a state appeared to encourage, having a monarchy really did have its advantages. In 1660, following years of exile on the continent, the dead king's son would be welcomed back and crowned King Charles II.

In this piece, I have deliberately looked to keep events and actions as streamlined as possible, because at its heart, this is a story about one remarkable afternoon in a tiny Cheshire village, and a tale that I hope has fired your imagination as much as it has done mine. The tale of the shoot-out, or at least the *hide-out* in the churchyard, should be seen as another fascinating piece of local history in the timeline of a village with a remarkable historical legacy.

The Civil War, in general, may be a story of division and brutality, but in moments like that which seems to have taken place at Great Budworth, we can also glimpse the humanity that is so often lost across the period. Beneath the colours of allegiance, the politics of both local magnates and men of more grandiose titles, and surrounded by the dangers of everyday life during the 1640s, there is still, at times, to be found a real human solidarity in our local stories of the conflict. They are not, for the most part, as eye-catching or enthralling to the casual history fan as the battles, executions, and scandals; for they are not to be as easily observed and digested.

There is no blame to be apportioned in light of this reality, it is simply that, as the old saying goes that 'sex sells', when it comes to history, nothing sells more than blood; nuance is often found to be a victim of the records that are written in the wake.

Yet here at Great Budworth, and the narrative implied by our tracing, and chasing, of the tale presented here, and irrespective of the divisions of the day, those Royalist soldiers that made their way to the village in search of refuge likely found, above all other things, the basic human kindness so lost in events of the period. Arriving in search of safety, however brief, and irrespective of consequence, it would seem that the villagers did their very best to provide it; and that, if nothing else, is something genuinely worthy of our commemoration today.

Above: Vale Royal Abbey today.

Below: Excerpt from *The Darnhall Custumal*.

Above: Sunrise over the fields at Eaton, a suspected site of Abbot Peter's murder.
Below: Original floor plan of Vale Royal Abbey.

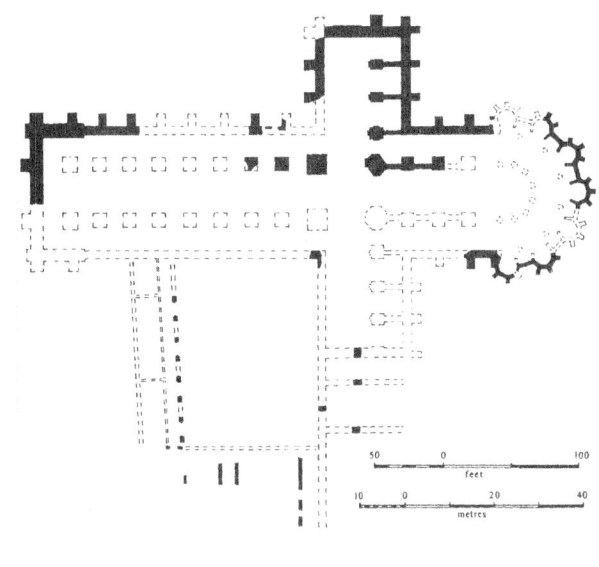

Above and below: Elevated ground and earthworks at the former site of
Shipbrook Castle.

Above: Shipbrook Bridge across the River Dane.

Below: Shipbrook's entry in *Domesday Book*.

Above: Ranulf Higden's tomb today in Chester Cathedral, set against a chapel wall following restoration work in the 1800s.

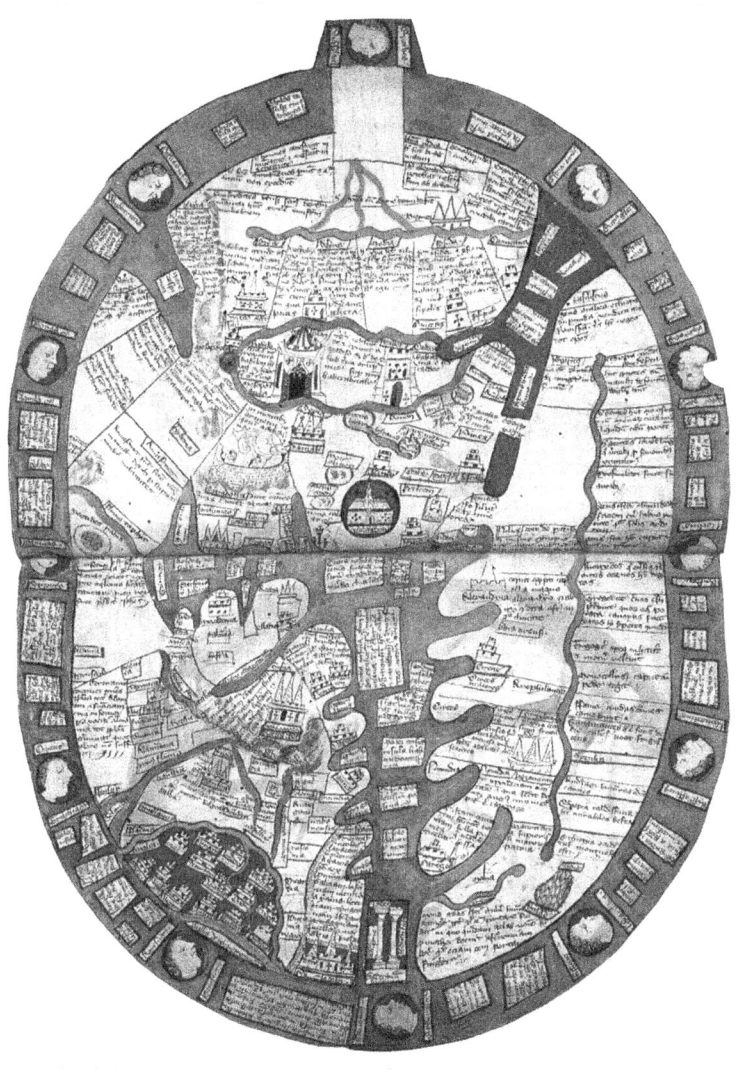

Above: Higden's world map from *Polychronicon*.

Above: St. Mary and All Saints Church, Great Budworth.

Right: The etched 'R' besides the schoolhouse door in the churchyard.

Right: Musket shot at St. Andrew's Church, Tarvin.

Left: Shot marks around the door of the schoolhouse at Great Budworth.

Above: 18th century woodcut of Robert Nixon.

Opposite (top): Title page from *Nixon's Original Cheshire Prophecies*.

Opposite (bottom): St. Chad's Church at Over, as featured in Nixon's prophecies.

Above: Marbury Hall in the late 19th century.

Below and opposite: Views of the Marbury Lady sculpture.

The Hungry Prophet

The Legendary Sale of Robert Nixon

The story of Robert Nixon, the 'Cheshire prophet' starved to death by the king, was once the best known legend of the county, retold and republished dozens of times across the eighteenth and nineteenth centuries. Precisely who the man was however, has always been something of a mystery, with many assuming he was little more than a fairy tale. Yet research suggests that not only was Robert a real-life figure, but that his bizarre and tragic end might just have been a reality too.

Born Under a Bad Sign

When her daughter was born in a cave during a thunderstorm just outside the town of Knaresborough in 1488, the fifteen-year-old Agatha Soothale could have held little hope for her survival, let alone have any aspirations as to what she may go on to achieve. The young mother had enough trials of her own, and now with a baby to cope with, the outlook was grim.

She was well known in the town but for all the wrong reasons; primarily that she had become influenced by the Devil and had seduced a local nobleman. For two years Agatha brought up her daughter in that cave, and no ordinary cave was it either. See, this cave, or rather the waters that ran along its walls and out into a pool beside its entrance, had a long history of turning objects into stone. If it were a story of fiction, not a better home for a 'witch' and her demonic offspring could you find.

Yet, when her daughter Ursula was two years old, kindness finally found the pair in the shape of the Abbot of Beverley, who dismissed any ideas of devilry and found Agatha a place at the Convent of St. Bridget in Nottinghamshire whilst placing the young Ursula with a local family in Knaresborough town. Briefly, things were looking brighter, but the legend of her mother soon cast a fresh shadow across Ursula's already troubled childhood. Only a few months after being placed in her new home, Ursula would climb out of her cradle and perch atop the fireplace, cackling. When she was a little older still, she was said to have somehow transformed the ruff on the neck of a man who was mocking her into a toilet seat. On another occasion again, she managed to manifest a pair of stag horns onto a man's forehead. Such is the bizarre and wonderful storytelling that folklore has left to us.

As she grew into womanhood, Ursula was increasingly taken by the woodlands around her and the natural potions the flora found there could create. As her interest turned into proficiency, the outcast child of Agatha Sootahle became a noted and respected herbalist, and come her early twenties she married, taking her husband Toby Shipton's surname. In the process, the name that history would remember her by was born. Mother Shipton had arrived, and soon too would the events that brought her to national attention.

When a neighbour knocked on her door and told her that someone had been into her house and stolen her new petticoat, Ursula informed her that she had the ability to 'see' who the thief was. The following market day, the thief - a local farm woman - arrived in the market square seemingly driven by forces beyond her control, dressed in the neighbour's petticoat, before involuntarily dancing around the butter cross, exclaiming her guilt aloud to all in earshot. Ursula simply looked on, her neighbour amazed at the power apparently in Urula's possession. As her abilities became well known, so too did the risks, and upon the death of her husband Toby in 1514, Ursula found herself holding the other side of the coin when it came to her reputation. Accused of his bewitching, she would move back into the woods, and the cave of her birth, to live out the rest of her days as a healer.

People would travel from Cheshire and Lancashire, even from as far away as Oxford, to meet the woman in the cave, for alongside her skill with herbs, and of course her apparent second sight, she had acquired a new power too. Ursula could see the future. So accurate was she said to have been that in 1537 King Henry VIII himself wrote a letter referring to her as the 'witch of York' and declared his ambition of meeting her; Ursula's visions of Thomas Wolsey and his power plays at court, together with her apparent inside knowledge of Henry's desire to break with the Catholic Church, doing much to prick the king's interest.

So well remembered was Ursula as Mother Shipton that the better part of 200 years on from her birth, the great diarist Samuel Pepys wrote that when looking over the damage caused by the Great Fire of London in 1666, the

Royal Family, with whom he was close, were keenly discussing Mother Shipton's foretelling of the event.

I myself have visited her cave in Yorkshire, where indeed the water does turn items into stone, or rather calcifies them due to its mineral content (not to spoil the fun). Nonetheless, there are dozens of cuddly toys, shoes, and even a few bicycles now 'turned to stone' and displayed around the place, the sight of which rightly creates a sense of awe in the visitors that stand and stare.

The story of Mother Shipton is probably the best-known such tale in Britain, concerning an outcast with apparently supernatural gifts and its the perfect backdrop from which to look at our own folk hero, and a story that in its way is just as wonderful and beguiling; the tale of Cheshire's 'Hungry Prophet' Robert Nixon.

One of the great charms of local history is the fantastical nature of the real-life characters and stories that it brings to the surface of the historical field, should we wish to look close enough. This is where those tales that would otherwise be deemed too incredible to be real, prove themselves. And in turn, they further prove just how remarkable our history can be. The story of Robert Nixon is, as such matters go, relatively well attested; that is to say, enough was written about him in the centuries following death, especially during the early 1700s, that we should reasonably assume the man actually existed. Or rather, at least some figure that latterly became known by his name.

That said, the very timeline of Robert's life, let alone the specifics of the events pinned across it, are still awaiting clarity. Opinion varies as to the time he lived, with the most popular views placing him either as being born around 1467 in Darnhall, the son of a farmer named John Nixon who leased his farm from Vale Royal Abbey, or alternatively around the year 1605, placing him as a servant of Thomas Cholmondeley, owner of that same abbey building during the mid-1600s.

It is quite the gap. Clearly, both cannot be correct, but if his 'real' life story is obfuscated, his legend is not, the key facet of which relates how Robert foresaw his own death, by starvation, when locked away in the court of the king. Which king this was though, is again contested. Richard III and Henry VII are variously mentioned in connection with the event, both of whom lived considerably earlier than the 1600s version of the tale; the version that sits best with Nixon's popularity during the eighteenth century pamphlet boom responsible for his legend's preservation. This piece will endeavour to sift through the trough of opinion, tit-bit, and speculation that comes with Robert, and look to build a clearer picture of the man in his true life setting.

How to Market a Legend

Following the invention of the printing press, or rather the industry around it that had developed in England during the Civil Wars, when arguments from each side would be printed as pamphlets, come the 1700s it had become fashionable to produce all manner of curious and titivating publications. As time moved forward, old stories would be rehashed and embellished, creating wondrous characters and tales to regale the people so interested. Much of Nixon's legend passed through this process, spurred on again into the 1800s as a result, where various books of his prophecies would be produced to intrigue and fascinate those who could afford them.

Here, we will peel through the pages written about Nixon at face value, as we look to understand the image of the man outlaid for us from the start of his legend. It is in the early stages of the pamphlet boom that we find our first recorded account of Nixon in *An Account of Nixon and his Cheshire Prophecies* from 1738, written by the historian John Oldmixon (born 1673). I have abridged the below only where not to do so would serve to obscure the story. It is the starting point of our journey;

> *Nixon was a short fellow, had a great head and goggle eyes, and used to slobber and drivel when he spoke, which was*

but seldom. He was very surly and would run after and beat the children that made sport at him. He would do nothing without beating. He had a large stomach and would eat up a great shoulder of Mutton at a meal. The manner of how Nixon was discovered to be a prophet, was this: His master being one day at plow, and Nixon following him, the boy stopped of a sudden, and dropped his bottle as if in a trance. They beat him but to no purpose, for he stood still for above an hour. At last, he told them, in a very rational manner, of things that were done some time before, and of others that would come to pass. Nixon, our prophet, was an idiot, and was employed by several farmers in Cheshire as their plowman. The noise of Nixon, at last, reached the ears of King James VI, who sent for him. But he refused to go, alleging that he would be starved. The king, being informed of Nixon's foolish refusal, said he would take care that he should not be starved and ordered him to be brought up to town. Now, that Nixon might be better provided for, he was ordered to be kept in the kitchen, but he grew so troublesome, licking and picking the meat, that the cooks locked him up in a hole; and the king, going suddenly from Hampton Court to London, meant they forgot the fool in the hurry so that he was starved to death at the king's court, as he had before foretold. There are diverse passages of our prophet's life and sayings transmitted from father to son in this county, to which, that when he lived as a farmer he gorged an Ox so unmercifully that one of the Plowmen threatened to beat him for abusing the beast. Nixon said that the beast should not be his master's in three days. Three days hence the lord of the manner came to claim the Ox. As whimsical as the account may seem to some, it was told to the Lady Cowper in the year 1670, by Dr. Patrick, late Bishop of Ely.

It would appear that just seven years later, Oldmixon produced another updated work on Nixon, *Nixon's Cheshire Prophecy at Large*, in which his original account had been built on further, the author having come across new information regarding Nixon's life. Here, his prophecies too were laid out, together with the following information;

This remarkable prophecy has been carefully reviewed, corrected, and improved from accounts given by our author. Robert Nixon, who was but a kind of idiot, and employed in following the plow. He lived in some farmer's families and was their drudge and serf. At last, Thomas Cholmondeley of Vale Royal took him into his house and there he lived where he composed this prophecy, which he delivered with as much gravity as an oracle, and it was observed that though the fool was a dribbler, and could not speak common sense, he spoke plain and sensibly. As credit to this prophecy, I dare say it is as well attested as any of Nostradamus or Merlin. Some ungodly people say there has been no witch since the Witch of

Endor, nor no prophet since Malachi, but it is plain enough that great men have in all ages had recourse to prophecy as well the vulgar fortune- telling….by the way, this is not a prophecy of today. 'Tis as old as the powder plot. I shall add a short account of his life…I could meet with but one man who remembered the prophet, and that was Old Woodman of Copnal. He says that Nixon was a short squab fellow, had a great head and goggle eyes; he was at first a plow for Farmer Crowton of Swonlow, and so stubborn that they could make him do nothing without any beating…the people it seems had a strange reverence for his stupidity and took his silence as portentous. The first time he was found to be a prophet was on this occasion. Farmer Crowton being one day at plough in the field, near the River Weaver in Swanlow parish, and his boy Nixon following him, the boy stopped all of sudden and dropped his bottle, and stood motionless with his eyes fixed towards heaven. Neither words nor blows could get him out of his trance for an hour. When he recovered, he took up the things he dropped and followed the plow. His master stood a while thinking him in a fit, but he did not fall. He seemed quite defensible of an alteration that had happened to him. For about a quarter of an hour, he talked very rationally about things that had been done and about things that were to be done; which made his master conclude Nixon's state had something sacred in it, and that his words were oracles.

Oldmixon was an English historian from Somerset, writing during the early eighteenth century, whose key works include *Critical History of England* (1724) and *History of England During the Reigns of the Royal House of Stuart* (1730). He was something of a dynamite figure to be taking an interest in such a character from Cheshire, and one for whom connections to higher circles of society were easy and plain. His writing is a great starting point in our search for understanding. Here, we find a very deliberately painted picture of Nixon as a 'village idiot' - to borrow a rather unsavoury phrase.

Odd looking and of a rather destructive and cruel nature, entranced during his work in the fields one day he began uttering visions of the past, present and future; an event that would ultimately lead to his summoning by the king and his death at the hands of the forgetful cooks.

Much like with Mother Shipton, at least in her youth, the picture is painted of a strange individual with a fearsome temperament. There is no mention of him being born in the 1400s though. That idea, despite being often mentioned in connection with Nixon today, actually comes from a much later publication that retrofits a prophecy of Nixon 'seeing' the Battle of Bosworth, the high tide of the Wars of the Roses, in 1485. It is nowhere to be found here, where he is very much a figure of near-history to the writers of the mid-1700s, from whom we also learn the names of several places and people into which we can delve later on.

The Prophecies

Whilst discussing the mystery of prophets we perhaps ought to take a look at their actual prophecies, and in Nixon's case, Oldmixon's earliest publications serve as the closest source we have as to what may have actually been said by the man. It is here that we find the charm of Nixon, and perhaps the reason for Oldmixon's interest. Far from fear, famine, and the kind of apocalyptic scenarios we may naturally attach to such utterances, and refreshingly free of any notions regarding the return of Christ - a classic feature of other figures in the tradition - Nixon's statements are fundamentally and fantastically colloquial. Here are the highlights which best help our understanding;

> *When a raven shall build in a stone lion's mouth on top of a church in Cheshire, then a King of England shall be driven from his kingdom, and never return more.*

A raven is said to have been built in a stone lion's mouth in the steeple at the village of Over in the forest of Delamere prior to James II being deposed in 1688.

When an Eagle shall sit on top of the house then an heir shall live to see England invaded by foreigners, who shall proceed so far as a town in Cheshire, but a Miller named Peter shall be born with two heels on one foot, and at that time living in a mill of Mr. Cholmondeley, he shall be instrumental in delivering the nation. As a token of truth of this, a wall of Mr. Cholmondeley's will fall, and if it falls downward the church shall be oppressed, but if upwards next to the hill at the side of it, then it shall flourish. Under this wall shall be found the bones of a British king.

Not long before the deposition of King James II, the wall on the Cholmondeley estate did indeed fall down, and upwards, which has been construed to hold relevance for the flourishing of the protestant faith under the incoming William of Orange. Elsewhere, in removing the rubble from the fallen wall, were found the bones of 'a large man' according to Oldmixon's own account. Additionally, an eagle was spotted at Mr. Choldmonley's house prior to William's taking of the crown. Regarding the miller named Peter, local lore shares that a boy was indeed reputedly born with two heels on one foot, in the parish of Great Budworth during the late 1600s.

A pond shall run with blood 3 days and the stone pillar

in the forest sink so low in the ground that a crow from the
top of it shall drink of the best blood in England.

Local folklore attests to a pond in Delamere which was
said to have run red soon after (likely as a result of mineral
content) and the old cross in the forest didi indeed sink
within a foot of the ground; likely due to natural
subsidence.

Whatever the truth of the prophecies and their coming to
pass, they certainly make for interesting reading. There is a
hint of a common pitfall in them too however and as we
delve deeper we should be mindful of two important
points when we come to discussing and integrating the lives
and prophecies of country prophets. More than anything,
across history, such figures have been used primarily as
political tools and religious totems, their prophecies -
whatever we come to make of the notion itself - being
recast, amended and, well, invented, in aid of the popular
causes connected to those behind their publications. The
apparent 'proof' of Nixon's prophecies being primly
centred on the events of the 'Glorious Revolution' of
1688, when the catholic James II was deposed by the
incoming, invited protestant house of Hanover and
William of Orange, should be, if not already, acknowledged
with a healthy dose of scepticism.

Harking back to a simpler, purer time of life is nothing

new either, and much in the way that such nostalgia can often find itself bewilderingly attached to political motivations, so too such sentiment was used in the past. That there were figures in the past of an era that seemed to have had the ability to foretell events in the future is a particularly useful tool with which to seek to influence the opinion of the reader; for if those prophets of the past forswore the ills of the day, they may too be able to tell folks precisely whom to blame for them

With this in mind, the quest of unraveling the predictions and prophecies attributed to any given figure is something of a fool's errand. There is just no way to know, and all the more likely, there is every chance that we are reading pure fiction. This is why I feel that particular section from the 1738 account is so useful. There's nothing extreme or political about it. It reads like folklore, and folklore can lead us to real places and people in such a way that so much 'official' written history cannot.

A central text to the legend that propelled Nixon to fame during the early nineteenth century and then on again into the age of the antiquarians, and one that we will glean much from on our own quest, is *The Original Predictions of Robert Nixon, Commonly Called the Cheshire Prophet* published by W. Minsull of London in 1800. Its core is taken from that 1745 account complied by John Oldmixon and its various republications, each of which enjoyed its own set of embellishments. One of these books contains a claim that its words were taken directly from 'Lady Cowper's correct copy'; Lady Cowper being named in the 1738 account as having direct conversational knowledge of Nixon's life.

By the 1820s Nixon had become a literal cartoon of whoever he really was in life, and this book contains a suitably outlandish image of him at its beginning, standing beneath a tree, looking rather stupid, with a skull at his feet; the implication being that Nixon's words included foretelling of both life and death. The work begins with a claim that 'what follows was taken from a descendent of this famous idiot, who at this time lives not far from Vale-Royal'. This line really brings home a connection with Nixon for me, as at the time of writing, I myself live in Vale Royal, and some may also think me quite the idiot!

I digress. Oldmixon then states that he had obtained an old copy of the prophecies that 'seemed to bear the appearance of antiquity'. It is here we get the first mention of Nixon belonging to the 1400s, with aeration that Robert was born at a place called Bridge House in the parish of Over, to a leasing farmer of Vale Royal, at Whitsuntide (7th Sunday after Easter) in the year 1467. It states here too that Robert was a challenging individual from an early age, and again the story of the Ox is relayed, before a series of prophecies are recounted attributed to this earlier, fifteenth century Robert. These include a foreseeing of the abbey at Norton and that at Vale Royal 'meeting' on Acton Bridge. Dismissed at the time, stones from both had actually been used in repairing the bridge in the years following the dissolution of the 1540s. Overall, the reformation of the church seems to be a central theme, with Nixon recorded as saying;

> *A time shall come when priests and monks*
> *Shall have no churches nor houses,*
> *And places where images stood,*
> *Lined letters shall be good,*
> *English books through churches are spread*

He is now a poet too it seems. It is in this work of the early nineteenth century that we get our direct reference to the Battle of Bosworth, when whilst out in the fields one day, Nixon is sad to have stopped working, taken out his whip, and begun lashing from one side to another exclaiming;

> *Now Richard! Now Harry!*
> *Get over that ditch and you gain the day!*

It is given that this outburst was then somehow relaid to King Henry VII himself by a circuit messenger. Nixon, apparently describing the situation at the end of the battle and something not commonly known outside of royal circles, was then summoned to court; at which Nixon said he would be 'clammed' - or starved - to death. For me, this story of Bosworth jars with the earlier prophecies recounted, which are deemed remarkable only by noting just how prosaic they are. This nineteenth century publication for the most part is designed to entertain, and whilst this could be said also of Oldmixon's 1745 publication too, albeit to a lesser extent, they are otherwise far removed. Oldmixon was long dead before these later publications ever came onto the market, his original work being re-cast into a free-for-all of myth-making and exaggeration.

Just how strange the uses of Nixon's name could be in relation to political lobbying of the day is something illustrated wonderfully well by the following account relating to a phantom battle being seen in Delamere Forest by locals during the early 1800s; an endeavour seemingly designed to tether an age-old Nixon prophecy concerning a battle in the forest to contemporary events in an attempt to stoke the fires of fear regarding a rumoured French invasion during the Napoleonic wars. I have included it here, as frankly, I think it is quite extraordinary.

As two ancient persons were walking over the said forest, to their great surprise, they saw at a distance before them an army rise out of the ground drawn up with their proper officers and their commanders in front of them, and whilst they were looking at and ruminating upon so strange a sight, to their most wonderful surprise and amazement there arose also another army out of the ground, at a small distance from the first, and farther in the forest, which was headed or commanded by a man in royal apparel, who, after having drawn up his army, marched to meet and engage the first; upon which a most bloody battle ensued with firearms, and many appeared to be killed on both sides.

A fifteenth century psychic, royal informant, or local 'seer' helping with his master's family matters and uttering curious predictions about children born with additional appendages? Real, fictitious, or somehow both, just how strange *is* the story of Robert Nixon when we place him alongside similar figures of the late medieval period, or perhaps crucially, the 1600s? Let us contextualise and consider, this seemingly strangest of tales.

Myths and Mystics

'Seers', meaning those individuals who claim the gift of seeing into the future, have been a common part of communities the world over for thousands of years. From ancient Egypt to Norse warrior culture and on through into the present day, such individuals have always been lauded and derided in equal measure. Most of us will be relatively familiar with Nostradamus, who recounted more than 900 prophecies during the first half of the sixteenth century. His level of fame is a rarity, but his profile, as an astrologer studying the heavens, is one with which we find parity among various others of the age.

William Lilly, an English astrologer of the seventeenth century, who was reprimanded for political predictions based on his work during the English Civil War, is reported to have predicted the Great Fire of London 15 years before it happened. Other names that we might class as 'seers' tend to be showered in religious rhetoric and ultimately feel more like mystics than 'genuine' prophets. Margery Kempe, a religious devotee from Norfolk, rose to prominence during the early 1400s courtesy of her 'conversations with God' as did Julian of Norwich, who spent most of her life alone in prayer as an anchorite locked in a cell on a bridge. Country 'seers' like Nixon would not have been all that rare, but it is rare that they are committed to record and remembered.

Both Nixon and Mother Shipton had interactions, we are told, with the kings of their day. That both are remembered with these events attached is likely the very reason their names have lived on at all. It is too perhaps the reason we should give thought to stories of their existence being genuine. Claiming to see into the future is a contentious business at the best of times, but there are a couple of serious considerations that come to bear on the idea at notably volatile junctures in English history. Diving the future is only ever one dodgy utterance away from being classed as witchcraft and such crossfire can be easily found in the record of English witch trials from the late sixteenth and early seventeenth centuries.

Mother Shipton appears to have been specifically known as the 'Witch of York' during her lifetime. Whilst such a moniker was never applied to Nixon, it is interesting to note that the nineteenth century writers on his life didn't seek to cast such a label upon him regardless. As a country mystic, which I feel is a better way to describe his character of history, we should perhaps think of him as more closely bound to the image of the fortune teller than that as a font of future knowledge. By all accounts, he didn't seem to have any particular control over the things he is reported to have said.

Nixon's story, and the way it has been constructed, speaks to me of a genuine historical figure; the colloquial nature of his predictions, together with the sheer weirdness of his death, combining to add a weight of perverse plausibility. Steering through the stories and commentaries then, it appears we have two possibilities for the 'real' Robert Nixon; a farmhand employed on the estate of Thomas Cholmondeley in the early 1600s during the time of King James I, or as the son of a farmer who leased a farm from Vale Royal Abbey in 1467, during the reign of Henry VII. Which then, is the more likely?

Sifting History

As we gather our thoughts in consideration of Robert Nixon's life, it is with a hope of discerning when that might actually have been in a literal sense. The best opportunities for answers are in the appraisal of his story's timeline(s) and the flowing current of his legend in the making. To this end, the facts bear out a surpassingly straightforward path.

Coming out of the 1600s, it seems that tales about a strange man from Cheshire with an ability to predict the future are doing the rounds amongst society circles, something no doubt aided by the assertions and 'proof' of his prophecies having being born out from the royal and religious events of 1688. By the 1740s, these tales have been brought together by the historian John Oldmixon and published, along with what is taken to be an account of Nixon's life, collected directly from locals in Cheshire.

At this juncture, Nixon is firmly placed as having lived during the early part of the preceding century, during the reign of King James I of England, which firmly dates Nixon's life to having ended at some point between 1603 and 1625, the period in which James I was on the throne.

Over the course of the eighteenth century, Nixon's story changes, growing in popularity far beyond his native Cheshire, which then results in numerous compendiums of his prophecies and life story being published. Drawing on Oldmixon's original work, but arriving in the 1800s in a much more elaborate fashion, he is now placed, for reasons we do not know, back in the 1400s. Key details are changed; he is now firmly connected to the Battle of Bosworth and King Henry VII and whilst I would struggle to call any eighteenth century account of Nixon's life a source in the traditional sense, in truth they are the best we have and they say nothing about Bosworth field. I think we can dismiss the idea of Nixon belonging to the fifteenth century entirely.

Focusing on the Nixon of the early 1600s, we have a number of other characters and places to consider for substance. As mentioned briefly before, we know the span of King James' reign and it gives us a window of 22 years in which he could have invited Nixon to court before inadvertently starving him to death in the kitchens. It is as we look further toward this, and consider the time and place of Robert's reputed master Thomas Cholmondeley, that things get very interesting indeed.

Following the dissolution of 1540, Vale Royal was effectively up for auction, and come 1544 it passed into private hands and a member of the Cheshire gentry by the name of Thomas Holcroft. Holcroft secured the former abbey and the bulk of its estate for £450 and then went to work on completely renovating the site, retaining only the central features of the old abbey - the cloister ranges and the monks' former dining hall - as he set about creating a new country mansion. Holcroft's line then continued to live at Vale Royal until 1615, when it came into the possession of the future Lords of Delamere, the Cholmondeley family, and in 1625 the estate would pass to Thomas, Nixon's aforementioned master.

It is events that took place 8 years prior however that really bare through onto our journey, for if we know that the characters connected to Nixon's story really did exist in the times and places needed to bed-in any plausibility to the wider story, it is in 1617 that we find an event that could tie everything - unbelievably - neatly together.

At this point, we can easily imagine a figure such as Nixon having been brought into the employ of Thomas Cholmondeley on the estate of Vale Royal, but we are still left with the issue of how such a figure could possibly come anywhere near to the king. In 1617 however. Mary Cholmondeley, the mother of Thomas, hosted none other than King James I as part of a hunting party visiting her

Vale Royal estate. Whilst there, James was so enamoured with his treatment that he personally knighted two members of the family. Furthermore, in an offer to boost the state careers of Mary's sons, he then invited them to court.

Vale Royal had long had a tradition of hosting royal hunts. That is to say, even prior to the establishment of the abbey in the late thirteenth century, there had been a hunting lodge in Darnhall (mentioned elsewhere in this book) that had hosted earls and kings on numerous occasions. As such, there is nothing coincidental about the encounter between King James and Vale Royal at all, and for a short while in the summer of 1617, both the king and Nixon would have been, quite literally, sleeping under the same roof.

From the first mention of Nixon in publication, the figure depicted for us was always a uniquely local one and the predictions said to have been made by him were concerning his local environment. That we then find the key characters in his story in play, factually, at exactly the place in history they were said to have been, should give us serious reason to think of Nixon the man as a real Cheshire resident of the early 1600s. The only leap then required to believe his story in a historical sense is to swallow the thought that he actually went to the court of King James I; something now seen to be entirely plausible in the context of accompanying Mary Cholmondelcy's sons. Given what we know, it would be far weirder, and virtually implausible, for all of this to have taken place as it did alongside a second, wholly fictitious yet perfectly matched, storyboard of events.

Perhaps James was regaled with tales of the local oddity in his midst. Maybe even in jest, he was brought forth to speak with the king. Let us not forget that James considered himself a real authority on matters of the occult. Perhaps Nixon fell into favour due to the more humorous side of his thinking on such matters. Either way, that some kind of meeting and acknowledgement took place is far from outlandish; that the king would then invite him to court is a possibility that has a myriad of avenues through which to have found itself born.

The story of Robert Nixon, one of the most curious and unusual figures in all Cheshire history is, at a glance, akin to something like a fairytale. The slightest of inquiries however pitches him firmly into the realm of folklore, with a healthy dose of suspicion as to his real existence to boot.

Pulling apart the strands of myth-making and hype that have served to smother his name courtesy of the early nineteenth century and its propensity for revisionist fantasy though, finds us firmly on a historical path. It is a path full of oddity, misunderstanding, and country mysticism that would deter most from looking closer still, yet when we do, we leave the story of Robert Nixon with the impression that in all likelihood, in early 1600s Cheshire, a remarkable if difficult young man had risen to local fame because of the wondrous and portentous things he said.

As a result of his unique nature, and likely too in no small part as a result of pity for his station, that same young man was then brought into the household of a wealthy family that, for a few days in 1617, entertained a royal hunting party on its estate at Vale Royal.

Just maybe that young man really did go on to starve to death in some lonely hole of Hampton Court palace too; his only crime, being notable enough to draw the attentions of a curious and inquisitive King James I.

A Ghost Story for Cheshire

The Bones of Marbury Park

The haunting of Marbury Park is one of Cheshire's most enduring legends of the supernatural. Most retellings however, if not all, have simply sought to repeat the basics of the tale without looking deeper into the history of the protagonists within. When we do, and look to consider the legend within the context of its earliest form, we find a very different tale to tell, and one that is all the more fascinating for it.

Memorial to a Haunting

As a nation, the idea of celebrated individuals being commemorated in the form of sculpture is something we're all quite familiar with. It is something many of us will likely take interest in when visiting a new town or a tourist attraction. Great kings cast in bronze perhaps, or decorated totems of human ingenuity remembered for their contributions to wider society; the memorialisation of our most noted historical personalities is a feature of almost every populated area across the United Kingdom. On occasion, we might already know a little about the subject too, be they Cromwell, Churchill, or Nelson, and sometimes we might even come across far more mythological figures, particularly in locations where the tourist trail is of notable financial value.

Just outside the entrance to Nottingham Castle, we find Robin Hood, bow drawn, forever set in that iconic, classic pose. Meanwhile, the eternal Peter Pan, cheerful and yet somehow aloof, plays his flute for the passers-by in Kensington Gardens, well within audible distance of his creator James Matthew Barrie's former home over on Bayswater Road.

In Cheshire, we're no different, although our statues and

monuments tend to have a more naturally local flavour. Viscount Combermere sits proudly atop his horse on a roundabout opposite the entrance to Chester Castle, the creation of the revered Franco-Italian sculptor Carlo Marochetti. Richard Grosvenor, Second Marquess of Westminster, whose family seat was at Eaton Hall in Eccleston, stands upon his pedestal of granite in Grosvenor Park, surveying the lands he gifted to the city in the mid-nineteenth century. Both are noteworthy, impressive creations, but how often do we really consider the life stories of the figures so remembered?

Combermere, a cavalry officer of distinction, serving with the Duke of Wellington during the wars in Spain and personally commanding the siege of Bharatpur in Rajasthan during the heyday of the British Empire, is now a much more contentious figure, his military prestige counterbalanced by his life as a slave owner. Grosvenor, an MP and Lord Lieutenant of Cheshire from 1845 to 1867 is remembered as a fierce patron of Chester and became popular in the city during his lifetime as a result.

Both are local icons of a Britain that saw such commemoration as a genuine honour. This piece, however, is an investigation into an altogether more modern sculpture, but one that tells a story that has seeped into local consciousness on account of it being connected to a more abstract kind of tale, being as it is, a memorial not to an esteemed local industrialist or military hero, but to a ghost.

Marbury Country Park near Northwich is a popular destination for Cheshire residents who enjoy its lime tree avenues, arboretum, and wealth of open space, not to mention its boating lake and open-air swimming pool. In a county filled with stunning country vistas and a substantial rural population, it really does take something special to create a formal space that can compete with the natural world around it. Marbury's location, nestled amongst the Mersey Forest, ensures it blends seamlessly with that stunning outer world.

Historically aware visitors however will note that the park's array of features haven't come about accidentally, but that they act as clues to its own distinct history as a private estate. It is on the boundary road of one of these features, the old walled gardens where vegetables for the grand house would have once been grown, that the focus of our quest stands today.

All year round people will come and go, enjoying their picnics and snowball fights, and whilst every visitor is bound to notice her, standing as she does over 20ft tall, few of them will know her story detail. Crafted from an elm tree that had died from saline poisoning, by the renowned chainsaw artist Simon O'Rourke, this figure of a woman wrapped in a shawl intrigues from very first sight. One side of her face is carved to look out towards the world, where she is pretty and hopeful. The other, windswept and sorrowful, stares back towards the site of the grand house she once called home.

The sculpture is a remarkable modern testament to the memory of a ghost story concerning the bleak fate of a maid from the hall who was in service during the early nineteenth century. It is a tale with several versions, none yet definitive, but all of which are known in some form across Cheshire. This is my attempt to cut to the heart of a story that has come to suggest adultery, murder, and even poltergeist activity. It's a veritable feast of love, loss, and the supernatural; the real tale of the Marbury Lady.

The Legend

As with many of our country parks, Marbury's origin lies back in the days of the grand country estates of the eighteenth century; estates with origins that came far earlier still, often being sprung from the later medieval period.

Marbury itself is an ancient settlement, recorded in the 'Domesday' survey of 1086 as *Merberie*, with a population of just 7 inhabitants. This fact betrays an often-quoted belief that the village owes its name to a specific family, which whilst not unheard of in the years following the

Norman conquest, shows that it existed before 1066, its name holding an Anglo-Saxon meaning for a fortified settlement near to a lake.

Although no traces of such a fortification exist today, when balanced against similar settlements throughout the region, we can assume that in all likelihood this was the forerunner of the first recorded dwelling on the site, which comes in the thirteenth century along with the first recorded church in the village. Throughout the later medieval period, the estate of Marbury continued to grow and would have needed to stand firm through various historical trials of the era in order to reach the other side in one piece. Some, such as the Black Death and the Wars of the Roses would have undoubtedly brought events and characters that are impossible to trace from our vantage point today, but others, such as the recording of 16 locals perishing from the 'sweating sickness' of June 1551, have come down to us relatively intact.

By the 1600s the Marbury family was a house of major sway in Cheshire, and as civil war broke out, Thomas Marbury, a former High Sheriff of Cheshire, declared for Parliament, going on to fight at the Battle of Nantwich in 1644. Richard Marbury, the last male heir of the family, would die in 1684, and having briefly been owned by General Richard Savage, the first noble to join the Prince of Orange on his landing in England in November 1688,

Marbury then passed (courtesy of a £21,000 price tag in 1715), to his son-in-law, James Barry, 4th Earl of Barrymore.

It is believed the timber-built house James brought had changed little since the Tudor period, and it was he who would rebuild much of it in stone, expanding the grounds extensively, with stables, courtyard orchards, and the first formal gardens being created under his stewardship. It is from the Barry family's time at the hall in which we find our era of intrigue, for it is events in the life of James Hugh Smith-Barry, who inherited the estate upon the issueless death of the 4th Earl's son Richard in 1787, that brings up the timeline of our tale as we find our starting point in looking for a 'truth' amongst the shadowy remnants of the strange stories associated with his time at Marbury Hall.

Smith-Barry was a renowned art collector, and at the time of his inheritance, had been living quite happily at nearby Belmont Hall in Great Budworth, which had been built by his father in 1749. The Barry family was of ancient Irish lineage and as a young man of considerable means, he had spent most of his twenties away from Cheshire, enjoying the adventure and highflying lifestyle so merited by the famous 'Grand Tour' of the day.

With its origins in the ancient European pilgrim routes, by the eighteenth century, the idea of a trip through Europe's most vibrant cultural centres, particularly those of classical Italy, was a major milestone in the life of most young, upper-class, European men.

Typically undertaken around the age of 21, this tradition flourished between the 1660s and the 1840s, when the invention of large-scale rail transport seems to have taken the shine off the trip as it became a far less exclusive affair. It wasn't all sightseeing and fine wine however, such continental tours had evolved to include a substantial educational element, sometimes lasting for several years, and offered a genuine route into the art and philosophy of the classical world.

For some, as with Smith-Barry, the tour would ignite a lifelong interest in antiquity and the period of the Renaissance; something that would inspire repeated visits throughout his life. He really had caught the bug, particularly for fine paintings and sculpture, and by his early thirties he had amassed an incredible private collection, with hundreds of pieces lifted from ancient Rome and Greece; more than 40 of them coming directly from the Parthenon frieze.

There were also to be found amongst his collection statues of Zeus, Livia, and a large number of Roman emperors. Many of these works had been acquired courtesy of business with the somewhat now infamous 'archaeologist' Gavin Hamilton, in an age when the legality of acquiring an ancient artefact was not viewed with too much moral sensibility.

It is from this period of art-sacking - essentially a process in which British and French archaeologists would uncover ruins of the classical world and then sell them to the highest bidder - from which many of our modern collections are born. As recently as 2021, legal cases and advisory requests have been brought in connection with such artefacts, with UNESCO getting directly involved with the British Museum in a bid to have the Elgin Marbles returned to the people of Greece.

Smith-Barry's time, however, was a very different one, and he would keep his collection in Belmont Hall until his death in 1801. It wouldn't be until 1856 that his collection would be formally moved to Marbury. For reasons that will become clear, it is this relatively well-attested record of international travel that has contributed to James Hugh Smith-Barry's connection with the more nefarious elements of Marbury Hall folklore that we will recount next. He was a man with a lifelong passion that will provide the springboard for our headlong dive into the entanglements of this supernaturally charged local tale; the legend of the Marbury Lady

The core tale of the Marbury haunting runs as thus. Whilst away on his travels, Smith-Barry fell in love with a beautiful Egyptian woman and before returning to

Cheshire, he had promised her that he would, in time, send for her so that they might spend their lives together in England. However, upon returning home, James found his father had taken steps to arrange a match for his marriage, and despite his initial protestations, he ultimately gave in to the sensibility of the age.

A while later, during an autumn storm, there was a knock upon the door of the hall. It was the Egyptian girl, who had made her way across the world to Cheshire. Upon arrival, she declared she wanted to act as a servant at the house and soon after, James and the exotic stranger fell in love all over again. As they loved in secret, a pact was agreed upon; should she die first, he would have her body embalmed and kept at the house in the hope that her soul would be with him forever.

In time, she did indeed die, and in some variants of the tale, pretty quickly, murdered by the lady of the house. In every version of the death, however, all tales dovetail that she was then duly embalmed and in accordance with the pact, kept at the bottom of the hall's spiral staircase in a chest.

Upon James' death in 1801, the body of the Egyptian servant was removed from the hall and buried in the churchyard at Great Budworth; at which point strange activity began to take place in the house. Cupboard drawers and doors would open and slam spontaneously, and villagers and servants both reported a 'misty' female figure floating around the gardens. Eventually, the decision was taken to bring the remains back to the hall - at which point the haunting ceased. Later, it is said the remains were then buried in an unmarked grave beneath the Marbury rose garden.

There is a lot to pick out from the tale, and several ways to read it. One is a simple ghost story. It is a great tale, and one that seems, at a glance, to have just enough provenance to chill the bones. Another way to read it however is to be found by studying the manner of the Egyptian woman's arrival at Marbury.

Finding her own way to Cheshire feels unlikely, especially if we are to place stock in her willingness to work as a servant; it certainly doesn't feel like an endeavour that a noble-born foreigner would readily undertake. It does, however, feel like exactly the kind of thing James may have arranged as a method of keeping his new mistress in his life.

There are enough localised, specific details to presume the tale has some basis in history too; the rose garden, the chest by the staircase. But perhaps the detail that ultimately, and most tellingly, will act as our route through the mystery, is that James Hugh Smith-Barry was very much the kind of man whose travels and interests would have brought him into contact with mummified Egyptian remains. It is also a tale that provides us with a range of questions we can pose to better traverse the realms of fantasy and reality. Was his father still alive during the period, and therefore actually able to arrange a marriage in his absence? Who exactly did James marry? And of course, we must ask, considering that we know he owned several alternative properties, if he was even living at the hall during the time in question.

These are the thumping beats we must examine in order to really consider the folklore at the heart of the tale - because from the present day looking back, the tale of the Marbury Lady is above all things, a rare and genuine example of embedded local lore. It is a story that has surfaced, and been nurtured by, an inherent local community. It is not, as so many of these tales can prove to be, just another regional variant on a well-known strand of rural lore that finds itself carried by travellers to new localities, only to spring anew in mildly altered states. So from the tale to the historical record we go, as we ask what do we *actually* know?

The life of James Hugh Smith-Barry, the art collector, is well established, but it is only due to the amount of evidence we have concerning the collection at Belmont Hall and latterly, the Marbury estate, that means we harbour enough certainty on the matter to run with. His travels and the assorted acquisitions made during his time in association with the local area around Marbury have left us with a number of contemporary accounts, in both antiquarian writings and more practical, simple catalogues of sale. Not least amongst them, a privately printed collection from his son's time at Marbury that was produced back in 1819.

Records of the collector's life give us several milestones by which we can guide our enquiries further as to the reality of his tenure. We know he was born in 1748, son of John Smith-Barry, Earl of Barrymore; but circumstances surrounding his family's standing at the time of his birth, and a little more helpful history, are illustrated to us further by the following entry in Robert Blacks 1891 work *The Jockey Club and its Founders* - the Smith-Barry's being serious players in British horse racing throughout the eighteenth century;

> *Mr. James Hugh Smith-Barry, born, in 1748, bore a name that tells still more plainly the story of his father's alliance with an heiress, who has been said to have married one of the two co-heiresses of the millionaire Mr. Hugh Smith, and is described as of Fota Island, County Clare, and of Marbury Hall, Cheshire. He seems to have been born about 1725, and to have died about 1784; and to have been a breeder, owner, and runner of racehorses on a large scale and with no little success.*

If his father died in 1784 as stated, when James was approximately 36 years old, we have a clear timeframe in which to place the events reputed to have taken place at Marbury. The estate had been in the family since its purchase back in 1715, and so would have passed quite naturally to James upon his father's death in 1784. Connecting this back to our legend of James returning to Marbury from his travels only to find that his father had arranged a marriage for him, we can say that, if accurate, that window is between circa 1770, when he was 22 years old and therefore of an age when such travels would have been undertaken, and 1784, when his father died.

In theory, this means the issue of the arranged marriage could be possible. That is, except for the fact that we know James never actually married anyone at all.

From his early twenties, and into his thirties, he spent as much time as he possibly could away in Europe and the East. It takes time to build up the knowledge, trust, and dare I say, love, required to curate such an extensive and renowned collection of antiquities. It is perfectly plausible, indeed likely, that this was a constant pursuit all the way through to the time of his father's death. We also know that six years after his father's death, around 1790, life had taken James on to Oxfordshire, and the purchase of Swerford Park, where he lived with his mistress Ann Tanner. Together, they would divide much of their time between his new Oxfordshire estate and his ancestral home at Fota, on the southern Irish coast. They would have 5 children together, all of which appear to have been legally acknowledged, and indeed it is their son who became heir to the family estates.

When James died in 1801, an annuity of £500 a year had been left for Ann and the children, but with the issue of her second marriage occurring just a year after his death, Ann was cut from the wider family, their children being placed with relatives back in Ireland. It is a period of the story that goes a long way to shaping our view of the legend's historical provenance. In reality, James spent very little time at Marbury. His will of July 1799 directed his collection to be moved from Belmont to Marbury, on account of him deeming the hall a more suitable location to house a formal gallery.

His only official time in residence at Marbury likely came between 1784 and 1790; something that rather dispels any notion of a love interest with an exotic Egyptian woman as per the tale. All in all, there is little to nothing of substance to suggest the story, in its popular form, has any founding in history. This is an outcome we sometimes find when following the trail of local folklore and legend, but one that can, as it does here, then cast an even brighter light across the core topic we are covering.

The popular legend of the Marbury Lady may have little

tether to historical reality, but that isn't to say that there isn't something to the narrative of the actual haunting.

The Box

So often with our local folklore, it is in the minor details that our route into the 'real' story is found; not in the headlines and neatly packaged narratives time carves out for us. The story of the Marbury haunting is not that of the popular tale. The dates, characters, and formulation of the timeline show nothing to suggest otherwise. For me, it is a story in the literal sense, a back-story that was likely developed during the early twentieth century as an expansion of what may now come to be seen as an even more curious reality.

This was an era in which ghost stories were very much in vogue. More precisely still, ghost stories of a very distinctive type. The story of the haunting of Marbury includes two elements that should be noted. Firstly, overall, the outline of the tale could be straight from the pen of that grand master of the English ghost story, M.R James, the gold standard writer of goulash delights from the period. James' stories are held in the highest of esteem today and many of them have been adapted for the classic, and at my time of writing resurgent, *BBC Ghost Story for*

Christmas. His ghouls rarely hit on the nose, and they're all the more chilling for it. They are odd and abstract, and many of them are tethered to ancient artefacts and discoveries made in the realms of high society. Often, they are directly connected to events in the lives of their protagonist. *Canon Alberic's Scrap-Book*, *The Mezzotint*, *A Warning to the Curious*, are all tales centred on unusual objects. There is even one tale actually called *The Rose Garden*. It is amongst this fine cannon of contemporary ghost stories that the haunting of Marbury could easily fit.

Placing this potential eventuality in the early twentieth century is something supported by the earliest references to the tale in literature. In the hundred years that followed James' passing, there is not a single mention of the tale amongst any of the antiquarian writings so popular in the period. It is only when we firmly prise the tale from the timeline that the possibility of a genuine origin begins to emerge, wrapped up in the linen with a body discovered in a box.

The story of the Marbury haunting reaches us in the latter part of the twentieth century, initially recorded by the king of 1970s paranormal writing Peter Underwood in his 1978 book *Ghosts of North West England*. Underwood took the collecting and retelling of ghost stories very seriously, not least in part due to his work as a parapsychologist and his position as president of the British Ghost Club for more than 30 years. His recording is the font from which all following versions pour forth; and when we strip away the direct association between Smith-Barry and the idea of a mistress from the East, we are presented with something else entirely. Free from the alleged adultery of our protagonist, we find a tale that, at its heart, describes how a body found in a box in Marbury Hall was acknowledged as the incubator for a plethora of supernatural goings-on in the house; a classic poltergeist case.

Now I am not to know the reader's position on matters concerning the supernatural, but for those who may be less inclined to indulge in such subjects, I would politely ask that they reserve judgement for the moment. This isn't simply a tale of things that go bump in the night and nor is it an example of the ridiculous demonic-centric situations that have been proffered and marketed by TV and self-styled 'ghost hunters' in more recent years. In truth, when dealing with history, we often find natural connections to the issue of ghosts, whatever they might actually be. I am always cautious to cross that bridge too readily. However, when it comes to the issue of poltergeist phenomena, taken as a whole, it is pretty damn hard to dismiss the evidence.

That James could have had human remains in a chest at Marbury is perfectly plausible. Egyptology was a very serious business during the period as an ever-growing fascination came with the discoveries made throughout the country across the nineteenth century. Following the invasion by Napoleon in 1798, and the discovery of the Rosetta Stone one year later, the floodgates opened on the topic for members of the European elite. True, James Hugh's time in the region predates this explosion by 30 or so years, but that there would have been Egyptian relics in the European market during his time as an active collector should be of little doubt.

Egyptian remains, bound in a casket, would be precisely the kind of treasure that the more curious side of his character would have appreciated. That some such object could then have been brought back to Cheshire, is highly likely; and it is exactly such a thing that was rumoured locally to have been found at the hall during its conversion to a country club in 1932. If true, this would directly account for the connection to an Egyptian woman found in the tale and provide the perfect inspiration for a fictionalised back story that has been handed down over the years since.

Noisy Spirits

First named so by Martin Luther, the sixteenth century protestant reformer and theologian, polter-geist in German, or noisy-spirit in English, is the name given to a type of phenomena that has been recorded with alarming consistency throughout human history. Today, many of us will associate the term with Hollywood movies and the like, but really, that is the somewhat sensationalised tip of an ice burg that poses very real and lasting questions for society's interaction with the topic. From the household spirits and fairy stories of European folklore to the more dramatic possession-based theories of the twentieth century, the plain truth is that ever since humans started to write things down, they have been writing about noisy spirits.

Tales of such hauntings have been recorded since at least 3500 BCE, with tablets in ancient Babylon, not to mention the ancient writers Pliny, Lucian, and Plautus all encountering spirits in their writings, but what is truly unique about the poltergeist phenomena is the consistant manner of the hauntings those spirits appear to inspire.

The banging of cupboards and doors said to have been reported by the servants of Marbury Hall is a firm staple of the poltergeist. And we should remember, back in the early twentieth century, when the tale seems to have been brought forth with those connections to the body in the box, this isn't something people widely knew. That the exact same phenomena had been recorded for thousands of years, all across the world (and relatively comprehensively since the 1600s) isn't something that could have been anything like common knowledge until at least the mid-1900s. It is perhaps the one area of the paranormal that poses a continually difficult question to the sceptic and for me, there are simply far too many corresponding accounts over years and cultures for it all to be part of some great hoax. Uncomfortable as it may be, it would seem, in some form, whatever it is, poltergeist phenomena really does exist.

Typically, the activity starts with a tapping. A noise, often described as 'coming from inside the walls' of a building. Strange events will be recorded; the sudden appearance of objects, or pools of water that cannot be accounted for. It will continue to build over time until the taps become much louder, even to the point of being audible in adjoining properties. Loud footsteps are common too, as too are the seemingly inexplicable occurrences of household objects moving on their own and doors and cupboards banging to and fro of their own volition. On occasion, this pattern escalates even further in a manner that suggests the energy is growing and taking on a more elevated, intelligent status. Voices may be heard, and in very extreme cases it seems, apparitions are seen.

Some readers will no doubt be familiar with the even more fantastical phenomena that is said to follow on again from there. In some cases, and again for reasons that appear very difficult to understand, the phenomena seems to be primarily focused on a lone member of a household, popularly given to be a young teenage girl. It is important to note, however, that before the internet age, before TV even, this stuff was mostly going on completely privately.

There was no gain to be made in a world that existed long before the notion of haunted tourism. Yet where the poltergeist was concerned, it was indeed going on in exactly the same manner as it does today. For the most part, this resulted in a real sense of terror and plight for those affected, accompanied by an all-encompassing desire that it just simply stop. In grand houses, servants would leave. In everyday residences, folks could be driven to the edge of madness.

A really solid example of just how this stuff could affect the lives of people connected to a property hosting a poltergeist can be found in a case from Hinton Ampner, now a National Trust property in Hampshire. A house thought so haunted it was unliveable, it is a case that contains a swathe of documentation by the family and several eyewitness accounts of very serious repute, not least among them Lord St.Vincent, Navy Admiral of *HMS Victory* fame.

It began in the 1760s, with a woman named Mary Rickets who lived in the house with her family. Again, it started with tapping before moving on to banging doors and cupboards; an activity which raised to such a level that Mary was convinced people must have been coming into the house at night. So distracting was the situation that the family put up a reward, equivalent to a full year's labourer's wage, for information leading to the arrest of the housebreakers. Of course, nothing was ever stolen.

The phenomena continued to grow, with a series of apparitions around the grounds, attested in Mary's diary, now in the British Library, along with notes on Mary's concern that her young children may soon see the ghost. So bad did the situation get that ultimately the family left, seeking sanctuary at the Bishops Palace in Winchester. As strange as it seems to say, a poltergeist at its worst should be seen more as a violent house invader than anything else.

In relatively modern times, the Enfield Poltergeist case of the late 1970s saw more than one hundred witnesses, including police and newspaper reporters, visit the Hodgson household as the children's toys flew around the room. Contrary to some reports in the years since the Hodgson family did not want to move to a new council house, and never made a penny from the story. Peggy Hodgson, the mother of the affected family, lived in that very same house until her death in 2003.

We could labour on similar cases for hundreds of pages, but rather, I would draw your attention, should you wish to delve further into the subject, to read Roger Clarke's excellent 2012 book, *A Natural History of Ghosts*. It is a work that can transform a person's view, should you wish to delve.

At Marbury, it appears the genesis of the story is the activity in the house, noted by the servants, together with the reports of the misty figures seen floating around the grounds. The remains in the chest drew suspicion as to somehow being the cause; the idea being that they formed the metaphysical battery by which the extreme weirdness was powered. On balance, throwing the damn thing out and into the nearby lake, a fate mentioned in several versions of the tale, might well have been the smartest thing to do all along.

A Different Haunting

In the tale of the Marbury haunting we have a looking glass into a period when life in both Britain and the wider world was in a state of real, irreversible change. In the pre-Victorian days of empire building, wealthy young men traversed the cultural highways of Europe with an air of expectation and privilege; a view that this was their very own, private 'university of life'. From it, great inspiration was taken, and great accomplishments were realised, but also there was an awful lot of cultural crime committed too, as items of antiquity were lifted into private collections without due authorisation or licence. This is also the era of slave ownership and educational patronage, which is often attributed to the same family at the same time, and a deeply problematic issue for us looking back today. But this *is* history. It is brutal and remarkable and at times, genuinely strange.

The Smith-Barry family, as we have seen, were major players on this stage, but their connection to Marbury, although significant, was not so much a love affair as it was a transactional means to furthering status. James seems to have been a man emboldened by his distinct cult of personality, spending far more time away from Marbury than within it. He is a man with a life story that, although perhaps viewed as unconventional today, is no less intriguing for our assertion that he did not in fact come back from his travels to engage in an affair with a mysterious visitor from Egypt. It is a great story, but little more.

Yet it would seem that at some point after his death, following the transferal of his collection to Marbury, strange events were witnessed by the household staff of the hall. From the view of folklore, without them, we are highly unlikely to have anything at all to create such a tale as the affair with the exotic mistress. His connection to the mysterious box shows well how these matters work out across the ages, but that such a connection between a location and the issue of haunting exists at all points to *something* occurring at the hall.

There are plenty of other ghostly tales up and down the

length of Britain predicated on similar, be them screaming skulls or ghostly footprints along ancient corridors, and it is this context that gives me some relative confidence in my understanding of how our tale of the haunting came to be so established. To take the reader with me on a trip into the territory of a poltergeist is not something I have done lightly, and I hope that my reasoning displayed here helps to show why I felt it nonetheless required. It is, I must confess for transparency, something I have - thankfully briefly - experienced firsthand. I too, simply wanted it to stop.

The recording in the folklore of cupboards and doors banging aloud without explanation is precisely the kind of everyday, trivial phenomena that, as these things go, tends to point toward some genuine event within the traditional nature of the phenomena concerned. If this element of the tale were to be as fictionalised as the rest, surely we'd opt for something a bit more noteworthy than some inexplicable banging around the house?

In recent years, the haunting of Marbury has become something of an easy ride on which to piggyback manner of supernatural vestments and claims. It is a genuine hope that this piece has flushed all that ghoul-baiting out a little, because within the story of Marbury is a genuine piece of local history with enough intrigue and oddity to make us ask questions enough; and through its semi-spectral veil, ponder matters that really do make us wonder. It is not only one of the most famous ghost stories we have here in Cheshire, but one that, when viewed through the recorded history of the phenomena at its heart, should perhaps be considered our most genuine.

King of Chaos

The Strange Lives of Samuel Johnson

An excerpt from *Mythstoric Origins - Exploring the Extraordinary Local Histories Behind the Legend and Folklore of East Cheshire, Peak District Derbyshire and the Staffordshire Moorlands*

The figure of Samuel Johnson serves to both intrigue and fascinate, but so little of his story has been properly examined that ultimately he is little understood beyond triviality. Seeking to address that balance by casting a light across the life of one of the most remarkable and bizarre characters in all of Cheshire history, we discover that sometimes the truth really is stranger than fiction.

In the Dark Wood

In a quiet corner of Cheshire, at a spot where the old village meets the new, beneath a dappled canopy of Beech leaves there lies a grave. Built in brick with an inscribed stone slab atop it, it rests in a woodland named after the man that lies within. This is the grave of Samuel 'Maggoty' Johnson, the reputed 'Last Jester of England'. But with his tomb, as with his life, things are far from what they seem.

There are some characters remembered to history in headlines and bold colours. Those who became synonymous with a certain event or time, forever crystallised alongside it. Famous, be it nationally or locally, they act as reference points for the ages. Others, edging more towards the circles of the historians, have been remembered by comparatively clear lines too; their connections to time and place, be them substantial or more obscure, nonetheless remain relatively easy to digest and understand.

Yet some characters act as a far more complex clockwork in the mechanism of their history. From one angle they may appear understood, but take the slightest sidestep, look again, and you will find that they have become unrecognisable. They are a myriad of avatars, and which one presents to us is entirely dependent on the portal we happen to be viewing them through; the complex, the difficult, the most human.

For most of us today, the identity of the man that was born as Samuel Johnson in Gawsworth in 1691 is almost entirely linked to that of 'the last jester'. A child-friendly cartoon that inspires local school projects and whose grave provides a curious distraction for passing ramblers. But this adopted moniker of the fool is mostly something we have ourselves bestowed upon his name, if for no other reason than it's the easiest option.

For many in the time of his life, depending on who you asked, he was variously known as a teacher, an actor, a writer; or perhaps it would seem, a madman. His grave itself is testament to the confounding nature of his life. The slab atop his tomb is inscribed, many believe, directly from his own dictation. Calling himself by both his birth name and his self-styled latter-day title of 'Lord Flame', it references the self-certified 'eccentrics of his genuis' and the small matter of how he is most definitely entering the afterlife as his master character of fire.

The fact that there is then a second slab, placed beside his table-tomb at some time in the nineteenth century, and which looks to address his memory with its own inscription in something of a mocking tone, only furthers the mystery of his legacy. We will come to view these inscriptions and their potential meanings later in the piece. Now though, which is not always the case, in order to gather the components of his life in a manner that may help enable an understanding of this most intriguing son of Cheshire, we must start at the beginning. The beginning of the unique and bizarre life-long riddle he has left for us all.

The Gawsworth Players

It is fitting perhaps that such an idiosyncratic figure as Johnson should be born to Gawsworth, as amongst all the great houses of Cheshire there is none to be found with a history more intrinsically entangled with rumour and intrigue than that of Gawsworth Hall. With only five families incumbent since the time of Norman settlement, Gawsworth is a bastion of our national timeline that serves as a truly fine example of manorial English heritage. The present hall, a Tudor master-build of 1480, complete with tilting ground and Elizabethan pleasure garden, has long inspired the idea that you cannot understand Cheshire without seeing Gawsworth Hall. Yet despite all of its attractions and delights, it would seem that Gawsworth Hall has something of a penchant for inspiring uniquely tilted events in the lives of those connected to it.

First, there's Mary Fitton, maid to Queen Elizabeth I, whose wild manner at court and scandalous affair with the

Earl of Pembroke saw her cast from the Queen's inner circle and reportedly provided the inspiration for Shakespeare's seductive 'Dark Lady' of the Sonnets.

Then enter Charles Gerard, a Royalist Lieutenant-General of the King's Horse and veteran of Civil War battles at Edgehill, Bristol, Newbury, Newark & Naseby, who ejected the Fitton's from the hall on his return from exile in 1662 on the strength of a claim that Alexander Fitton's original inheritance was based on a forged document. Most fascinating of all though is perhaps the situation that arose upon the death of the 3rd Earl of Macclesfield in 1701.

With no natural heir to the estate, Gawsworth was left to a niece, a certain Lady Mohun. Contested by another potential heir in the form of the Duchess of Hamilton, the feud raged on until 1712 when the ladies' respective husbands - Lord Mohun and the Duke of Hamilton - took the dispute to its ultimate conclusion and killed one another in a pistol duel in Hyde Park. It was an event of such note that in its wake, Queen Anne herself campaigned for a ban on such means of violent resolution. It is a fitting backdrop of events from which to begin our tale of Samuel Johnson, as whilst Johnson was himself no patron of Gawsworth Hall, it would seem the hall had a guiding hand in his rather marvellous journey from the very start.

Dancing Master Johnson

Parish records show that Samuel Johnson was christened at St Micheal's in Macclesfield in December of 1691. The son of one Joannis Johnson, it is the only record pertaining to Johnson's birth that fits the timeline. Confirming his birth is something that can never be taken for granted, but from that winter's day Christening, we can begin to look through the winding path of his life and attempt to unravel the mystery of the man. Compared with those of the people he would come to be so well connected with, these were genuinely humble beginnings. How such a child was able to rise to a position whereby his claim of being the last jester in England was accepted to posterity is a considerable question to pose.

In essence, there are two distinct types of jester present throughout history. The 'Natural Fool' would be an individual seen, by opinion of the time, to be naturally suited to the role by virtue of physical deformity or mental state, whereas the perhaps more rounded and ultimately vocational role of 'Licensed Fool' is that which should be more closely associated with Johnson; think more paid comic of the court than physical curiosity.

Ultimately, however, whether a natural or licensed fool, the position of court jester was far from a laughable appointment. Often on a par with members of the court's inner circle such as Ladies-in-Waiting, the role of the jester can trace its roots back to the courts of ancient Egyptian Pharos and Chinese Emperors. Beyond the more obvious acts of comedy performance, drama and musicianship, the jester could be relied upon - in fact, encouraged - to speak freely; the assumption granted that the fool's way with words would provide a far more palatable manner in which to point out any folly in their master's plans.

Bad news too, so often a dangerous and deadly burden to bear, was often left to the breaking of the jester; something brilliantly illustrated here in an account from fourteenth century France. Following the destruction of his fleet by the English at the Battle of Sluys in June 1340, it is reported that Phillip VI of France was given the news of defeat by his jester, who burst into his presence with a series of exclamations;

> *The cowardly English! The bastard English! The faint-hearted English!*

When the king asked why the jester was so negative in his opinion of the English character, the jester supposedly replied;

> *Because they would not jump out of their ships into the sea as our brave Frenchman did!*

Such access to power naturally brought its privileges too. Will Sommers, jester to Henry VIII appears to have grown so close to the king that Henry felt it fitting to include him in the 1545 portrait *Henry the Eighth and His Family,* alongside his former wife Jane Seymour, his daughters Mary and Elizabeth, and son Edward. But Johnson was not the fool of a monarch. There is no reference to him in connection with the kings of his lifetime, George I, II, and III respectively. So if he was to be 'the last jester' it was in the court, or perhaps to be more accurate, in the pay, of a patron outside of Royal circles. Enter the Duke of Montegu.

Making an Impression

John Montagu, 2nd Duke (otherwise known as both Viscount Monthermer and Marquess of Monthermer thanks to the intricacies of the British nobility system) was something of an eighteenth century celebrity. Born in 1690, by fifteen he was already deemed fit to partake in a Grand Tour of the continent, something usually reserved for young upper-class men in the early twenties, and was soon married to Lady Mary Churchill, daughter of the Duke of Marlborough, and part of one of the most powerful families in the burgeoning British Empire.

Come 1722 and we find Montagu as governor of Saint

Lucia and Saint Vincent in the West Indies, and in the throws of a time that he appears to have spent indulging in sponsorship of naval adventuring, courtesy of his appointment of the merchant, Nathaniel Uring, as deputy.

Uring, who was sent to sea with seven ships at Montagu's behest with the intention of creating further new British colonies in the Americas, ultimately failed in his pursuits, his endeavours often checked by French troops present across the region in a game of naval cat and mouse that many wealthy members of the British nobility were wanton to undertake, on the chance that one would come good in their name. This tale of chance is important, as it gives an insight into Montagu's adventurous character. His desire perhaps, to play the imperialist. The kind of chap that may consider his inner circle something of an imperial court.

At the point of Montagu's Caribbean adventuring, Johnson's own career had already achieved enough lift to mark him out as a remarkable man, as we know that come the early years of the 1720s he had achieved a status of Dancing Master to Manchester's more affluent middle-class families. This, from his birth in Gawsworth to a local family without title, is striking enough to wonder if there may have been something in Johnson's lineage that allowed him to make such deft moves in society via sponsorship. After all, this is a young man that appears born into a rural life of farm work and manorial support. To move into the arts without a helping hand demonstrates a possession of serious natural talent.

Johnson's profession, which involved him teaching the dances and entertainment of courtly settings to those families wishing to make entry into such circles, naturally brought him into contact with all manner of characters from Georgian high society. Such was Johnson's standing within that world that in 1722, the same year as Montegu became governor in the West Indies, he curated a ball in Manchester that was attended by none other than the esteemed poet, John Byrom. Johnson's star, however humble of origin, was definitely on the rise, and by 1724 his abilities in dance and as a master fiddle player had taken him to London. The move would change Johnson's life forever.

The Birth of Lord Flame

When the Theatre Royal Haymarket opened on December 29th, 1720, it was just the third public theatre in the now world-famous West End of London. Its debut performance was the privilege of a group known as *The French Comedians of His Grace the Duke of Montague* and their play *La Fille a la Morte, ou le Badeaut de Paris (The Dead Girl of Paris),* and would place it at the heart of the emerging theatre scene in an area of London that had previously been more used to seeing the sight of hay carts blocking the market roads than French actors drifting across it's streets. Indeed, so noted upon was the company that had provided the theatre's first performance that for several years the venue was known by many as simply 'The French Theatre'.

The theatre's first major success however would come courtesy of a play written by Johnson - following a meeting with the Duke - whose patronage of the theatre is born out in the name of that opening French troupe. It is at this point that we might recap Johnson's life before things get genuinely strange; a Gawsworth boy of supreme artistic talent and the force of character to establish himself as a serious contender in the artistic circles of society.

In April 1729 Johnson's play, *Hurlothrumbo or The Supernatural* ran for thirty consecutive nights at The Theatre Royal. Johnson was also the main star, singing, dancing, playing the fiddle, and for much of it, all whilst wearing stilts. His character's name, Lord Flame, was a kind of high king of chaos and seemed to have awoken something in Johnson's soul. Something that would never leave again.

If that sounds to you like a somewhat bizarre spectacle to behold, you're not alone. An 1855 remembrance of the play stated that, 'a more curious or insane production has seldom issued from the human pen'; not that

Hurlothrumbo's artistic insanity was seen as a negative in the time of its setting. Rather, if anything, the spectacle appeared to cast something of a spell. The theatre was packed to the rafters each night with some of the most influential and fashionable celebrities of the day in attendance, creating an audience that, it is said, quite literally applauded the piece from beginning to end, every single night.

The so-called 'nonsense play' feels like a forerunner of Monty Python and a piece that contained such wonderfully insightful dialogue as 'this world is all a dream, and outside, a dunghill pav'd with diamonds' and 'rapture is the egg of love, hatched by a radiant eye'. A particular section of revelation seems to have involved the singing of a song that hoped to inspire the king to make himself a cocktail of gunpowder and brandy.

In the wake of the play's success, it would become satirised in popular culture in that manner that denotes true cultural impact. It was referenced in Henry Fielding's play *Authors Farce* that very same year, and again twenty years later in his novel *Tom Jones*, where the insanity of the play is illustrated by reference to Johnson himself in a passage that reads;

> *…thus the famous author of Hurlothrumbo told a learned bishop, that the reason his lordship could not taste the*

excellence of his piece was, that he did not read it with a
fiddle in his hand; which instrument he himself had
always had in his own, when he composed it.

Copies of the play would be found in many esteemed residences; Lord Walpole, one of the most prominent politicians of the day, reportedly ordered no less than 30 copies, each signed by the author.

The theatre's connection with the Duke of Montagu had brought Johnson to the attention of a patron, and for the next decade, Johnson became a serious fixture in the world of London theatre. Further productions would hit the stage; *The Mad Lovers*, *All Alive and Merry*, a comic opera called *A Fool Made Wise* and a tragedy entitled *Pompey The Great*.

Other connected pursuits would come to Johnson's door too, all equally bizarre. It is Johnson who is believed to have been behind the publishing of *The Merry Thought,* a collection of graffiti and poetry lifted from the alehouse windows and public latrines of London.

Yet whereas *Hurlothrumbo* had been both a theatrical phenomenon and a published success, Johnson's follow-ups were not. Over time, the life he had left as a dancing master in Manchester seemed to become the more viable one once more, and by the mid-1740s, his theatre career waining, he was back in Cheshire.

Maggoty Brains

Returning to Gawsworth, Johnson appears to have been given provision to live at the hall. His private audiences for local gentry showed his talents to be far from dimmed and in the guise of the performing Lord Flame, he was still something of a sensation. It seemed that playing the character enabled Johnson to relive his glories, maybe even build new ones. For such a precocious mind, it was only a matter of time before Lord Flame took over entirely.

It is from this time, coupled with his earlier patronage by Montegu, to which I believe the idea of 'The Last Jester' belongs. As at Montegu's discretion earlier in his life, Johnson's talent as Lord Flame afforded him a life of performance and patronage back at Gawsworth.

There are some resources online that place Johnson as an inhabitant of the hall itself, but this seems very unlikely. The duel of 1712 left the estate in the hands of the Gerards, until William Stanhope, 1st Earl of Harrington, purchased it later in the eighteenth century, and it remained with the family until 1935. Much more likely is that Johnson was accommodated on the property as part of his deal as in-house performer, a period that would consist of the last thirty years of his life, and in which Johnson's actions in the village appear to have grown steadily stranger.

Rumours as to the nature of Johnson's private life soon began circling back in Gawsworth. A mysterious female companion had joined him; and one that had more than a passing resemblance to the infamous 'Dark Lady' herself. He wandered abroad at night in the woods as Lord Flame; his performance skills rumoured to be enabled by some strange magic. Not all locals thought it quite so esoteric, however, explaining Johnson's lifestyle away far more prosaically. Johnson they said, had 'maggots in his brain.' And so, the image of 'Maggoty Johnson' was born.

At some point toward the end of his life, Johnson is said to have fired an arrow from the rooftop of New Hall, the Georgian manner house built for Lord Mohun in 1707, his stated desire being that he be buried in a tomb where it landed. That spot is the plot now known as Maggoty Woods and that grave, courtesy of the words implied to have been ordered by Johnson himself, grants us a snapshot of the view the man had of himself.

This, and its strange counterpart that appears in the following century, combine into a conundrum that, whilst at first, may well seem to offer us further insight into the strange and wonderful lives of Samuel Johnson, upon study feels rather more like his final joke. His own inscription, a riddle of his life, reads as follows;

Under this Stone

Rest the Remains of Mr SAMUEL JOHNSON

Afterwards ennobled with the grander Title of

LORD FLAME

Who after having been in his Life distinct from other

Men

By the Eccentricities of his Genius

Chose to retain the same Character after his

Death And was, at his own Desire, buried here May

5th A.D. MDCCLXXIII aged 82.

"Stay, thou whom Chance directs or ease persuades,

To seek the Quiet of these Sylvan shades

Here, undisturbed and hid from Vulgar Eyes

A Wit, Musician, Poet, Player, lies

A Dancing master too in Grace he shone

And all the arts of Opera were his own

In Comedy well skilled he drew Lord Flame

Acted the Part and gaind himself the Name

Averse to Strife how oft he'd gravely say

These peaceful Groves should shade his

Breathless Clay

That, when he rose again, laid here alone

No friend and he should quarrel for a Bone

Thinking that were some old lame Gossip nigh

She possibly might take his Leg or Thigh"

What are we to take from this testament? It is clear that the story of Johnson choosing the woods as his burial plot seems indeed to be the case. His concern with confusion over his bones being mistaken for someone else has often been put down to the idea that he had been buried in the local church prior to re-internment in the woods, but again, this seems unlikely. Indeed the county burial register names the woods as his burial spot. Perhaps the inscription was always designed to have people like us searching in vain for meaning to his madness some two hundred and fifty years later. It certainly keeps us talking about Lord Flame. If so, it was a trick that not everyone seems to have appreciated.

At some point following his death, a second, more curiously cautionary inscription was placed at the site by a third party. It is believed by some that this second slab and inscription was laid at the request of Lady Harrington (whose family name has been adopted by the local pub), with the aid of Rev. Edward Massey, in order to 'balance out' the humour of Johnson's own dictation. Reading the lines, however, one would be forgiven for sensing a deeper motivation at the root of the addition. A warning of sorts;

If chance hath brought thee here, or curious eyes
To see the spot where this poor jester lies
A thoughtless jester even in his death
Uttering his jibes beyond his latest breath

O stranger pause a moment, pause and say:
"Tomorrow should'st thou quit thy house of clay
Where wilt thou be my soul? in paradise?
Or where the rich man Lifted up his eyes
Immortal spirit would'st thou then be blest
Waiting thy perfect bliss on Abraham's breast
Boast not of silly art or wit or fame
Be thou ambitious of a Christian's name
Seek not thy body's rest in peaceful grove
Pray that thy soul may rest in Jesus love
O speak not lightly of that dreadful day
When all must rise in joy or dismay
When spirits pure in body glorified
With Christ in heavenly mansions shall abide
While wicked souls shall hear the Judges boom
"Go ye accursed into endless gloom"
Look on that stone and this, and ponder well
Then choose twixt Life and Death,
Heaven and Hell'

The Last Laugh

Samual Johnson's resting place comes today complete
with the standard palate of ghost sightings and spooky
inclinations that you might expect, including the classic 'say

his name three times and he will appear'. I suspect he'd have quite liked that. One suspects he'd have quite liked the confusion the second slab has added to his story too.

His grave is, on the surface, a curious local monument to a local figure who has somewhat affectionately become known as 'Maggoty Johnson'. Beneath the facade, however, lies a story of incredible progress and social mobility. A crash-map of success and indulgence, talent and fortune. A truly unique life lived.

Ultimately, we will never quite know exactly who we should be commemorating there. Is it the dancing master, the humble local who through force of talent and luck of connection rose to inhabit the lofty social circles of Manchester? The playwright and actor, that took an emerging London theatre scene by storm with his eighteenth century, 'Pythonesque' insanity shows? The more serious writer, working from the fringes of the literary world as he fought a losing battle with the brilliance of his mind? Or perhaps it really is simply the jester; the hired, entertaining hand who would perform on cue for the great and good of high society. That is our choice to make. Our opinion to express, and a question I dare say that folks will be pondering long after you and I are gone. Maybe we should just take Maggoty's word for it, for as far as he was concerned, the answer is clear.

It may have been Samuel Johnson who was born in the

village of Gawsworth back in 1691, but the man that was buried there on the 5th May 1773 was very definitely, Lord Flame.

Mythstoric Origins contains essays regarding the historical provenance of legend and folklore inherent across East Cheshire, Peak District Derbyshire and the Staffordshire Moorlands.

A Cestrian Song

Further Reading

Memorials of the Civil War In Cheshire and the Adjacent Counties (Thomas Malborn, 1889)

East Cheshire Past and Present (J,P Earwalker, 1877)

The History of Cheshire Containing King's Vale-Royal Entire (John Pool, 1778)

The History of the County Palatine and City of Chester (George Ormerod, 1819)

The Ledger-book of Vale Royal Abbey (Manchester Record Society, 1914)

Domesday Book (Williams and Martin, 2003)

Polychronicon (Oxford Library, 2000)

Magic in the Cloister (Sophie Page, 2013)

Nixon's Original Cheshire Prophecy (John Oldmixon, 1838)

A Natural History of Ghosts (Roger Clarke, 2012)

Full source list and image credits available upon request from thelocalmythstorian@yahoo.com

About the Author

Eli Lewis-Lycett is a local history researcher, writer and podcaster living in Cheshire. He is the founder of *The Local Mythstorian* project, regular contributor to *Haunted Magazine* and folklore columnist for *Cheshire Life Magazine*.

He also enjoys speaking on matters related to local history and folklore at events across Cheshire, Derbyshire and Staffordshire.

Visit **thelocalmythstorian.com** or for more orginal content regarding the local history and folklore of Cheshire, Derbyshire and Staffordshire.

@TLMythstorian
thelocalmythstorian@yahoo.com

Printed in Great Britain
by Amazon

39005066R00128